THE IMPORTANCE OF

Albert Einstein

by
Clarice Swisher

Lucent Books, P.O. Box 289011, San Diego, CA 92198-9011

These and other titles are included in The Importance Of biography series:

Cleopatra	Margaret Mead
Christopher Columbus	Michelangelo
Marie Curie	Wolfgang Amadeus Mozart
Thomas Edison	Napoleon
Albert Einstein	Richard M. Nixon
Benjamin Franklin	Jackie Robinson
Galileo Galilei	Anwar Sadat
Thomas Jefferson	Margaret Sanger
Chief Joseph	Mark Twain
Malcolm X	H.G. Wells

Dedication

For Karin and Annie

Library of Congress Cataloging-in-Publication Data

Swisher, Clarice, 1933-
    Albert Einstein / by Clarice Swisher
    p. cm.—(The Importance of)
    Includes bibliographical references and index.
 Summary: A biography of the scientist famous for his theory of relativity.
    ISBN 1-56006-042-5
    1.Einstein, Albert, 1879-1955—Juvenile literature.
 2. Physicists—Biography—Juvenile literature. [1. Einstein, Albert, 1879-1955. 2. Physicists.] I. Title. II. Series.
QC16.E5S97   1994
530'.092—dc20   93-17280
[B]   CIP
                                                               AC

Contents

Foreword

THE IMPORTANCE OF biography series deals with individuals who have made a unique contribution to history. The editors of the series have deliberately chosen to cast a wide net and include people from all fields of endeavor. Individuals from politics, music, art, literature, philosophy, science, sports, and religion are all represented. In addition, the editors did not restrict the series to individuals whose accomplishments have helped change the course of history. Of necessity, this criterion would have eliminated many whose contribution was great, though limited. Charles Darwin, for example, was responsible for radically altering the scientific view of the natural history of the world. His achievements continue to impact the study of science today. Others, such as Chief Joseph of the Nez Percé, played a pivotal role in the history of their own people. While Joseph's influence does not extend much beyond the Nez Percé, his nonviolent resistance to white expansion and his continuing role in protecting his tribe and his homeland remain an inspiration to all.

These biographies are more than factual chronicles. Each volume attempts to emphasize an individual's contributions both in his or her own time and for posterity. For example, the voyages of Christopher Columbus opened the way to European colonization of the New World. Unquestionably, his encounter with the New World brought monumental changes to both Europe and the Americas in his day. Today, however, the broader impact of Columbus's voyages is being critically scrutinized. *Christopher Columbus,* as well as every biography in The Importance Of series, includes and evaluates the most recent scholarship available on each subject.

Each author includes a wide variety of primary and secondary source quotations to document and substantiate his or her work. All quotes are footnoted to show readers exactly how and where biographers derive their information, as well as provide stepping stones to further research. These quotations enliven the text by giving readers eyewitness views of the life and times of each individual covered in The Importance Of series.

Finally, each volume is enhanced by photographs, bibliographies, chronologies, and comprehensive indexes. For both the casual reader and the student engaged in research, The Importance Of biographies will be a fascinating adventure into the lives of people who have helped shape humanity's past, present, and will continue to shape its future.

Important Dates in the Life of Albert Einstein

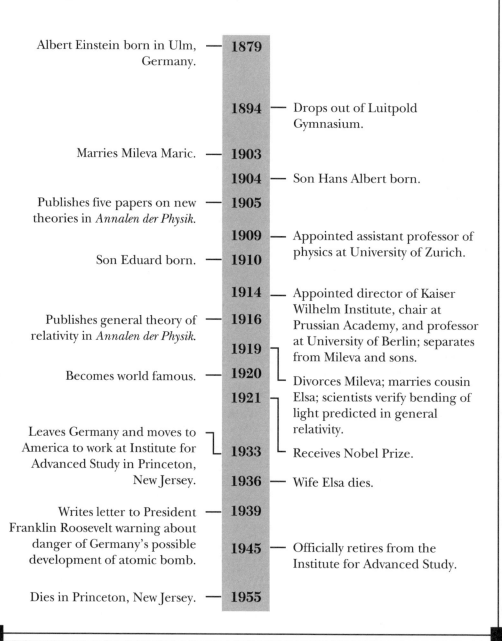

Albert Einstein born in Ulm, Germany. — **1879**

1894 — Drops out of Luitpold Gymnasium.

Marries Mileva Maric. — **1903**

1904 — Son Hans Albert born.

Publishes five papers on new theories in *Annalen der Physik*. — **1905**

1909 — Appointed assistant professor of physics at University of Zurich.

Son Eduard born. — **1910**

1914 — Appointed director of Kaiser Wilhelm Institute, chair at Prussian Academy, and professor at University of Berlin; separates from Mileva and sons.

Publishes general theory of relativity in *Annalen der Physik*. — **1916**

1919

Becomes world famous. — **1920**

Divorces Mileva; marries cousin Elsa; scientists verify bending of light predicted in general relativity.

1921

Leaves Germany and moves to America to work at Institute for Advanced Study in Princeton, New Jersey. — **1933** — Receives Nobel Prize.

1936 — Wife Elsa dies.

Writes letter to President Franklin Roosevelt warning about danger of Germany's possible development of atomic bomb. — **1939**

1945 — Officially retires from the Institute for Advanced Study.

Dies in Princeton, New Jersey. — **1955**

Revolutionizing Science

Albert Einstein developed theories in the first decades of the twentieth century that overturned a two-hundred-year-old view of the universe and changed the course of physics. For two hundred years, the world had accepted English physicist Isaac Newton's theory of motion as the right way to

Albert Einstein writes out the equation expressing the density of the Milky Way galaxy on a blackboard at the Mount Wilson Observatory in Pasadena, California. His ideas revolutionized the science of physics.

measure things in time and space and upheld his theory that gravity held the universe in order. When Einstein went to school, he learned these accepted theories.

In 1905, at the age of twenty-six, Einstein published several theories. One showed that light is made up of tiny particles. Another proved that atoms exist. His relativity theory showed a way of measuring things that overturned Newton's way. In 1916 Einstein showed that Newton's theory of gravity was inaccurate and provided a new theory in its place. Just one of these theories would have changed physics in the twentieth century, but Einstein developed several revolutionary theories. Einstein's contributions to science are so important that a joke among scientists asks "Who is the most famous scientist after Einstein?" And the answer is "Einstein."

In his early life, it would have been difficult to predict that Einstein would make such a large impact on the world. As a child he was slow learning to talk. He did poor work in his classes, quit violin lessons, and dropped out of school. He failed the university entrance exams the first time he took them and later had problems getting a job. Many times he failed because he stubbornly insisted on studying his way instead of someone else's.

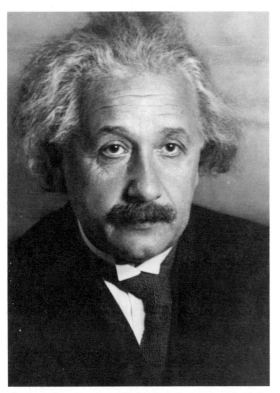

German-born genius Albert Einstein is recognized the world over, but not everyone knows that he was also a philosopher and humanitarian.

But this stubbornness and independence of thought left him free to pursue his questions about the universe and develop them into theories, independent of other scientists and their ideas.

When Einstein published his first theories, he was unknown to other scientists. He had been an average student at the university and had taken a job as a clerk in an office, away from all scientific activity. After 1905, however, a few scientists recognized the importance of his theories, and Einstein gradually received job offers from universities. When he was invited to direct a scientific institute in Berlin, Germany, he had reached the top of his field. He held this position for nearly twenty years.

Einstein also took an interest in humanitarian causes. He was a pacifist who worked hard to promote world government. He helped Jews establish a homeland in Palestine. And he worked to insure that scholars had the freedom to think independently and do their work without political interference. After he achieved fame, he felt compelled to use his influence to further the causes he believed in.

One of Einstein's biographers, Phillip Frank, said that "anyone who comprehends even a little of Einstein's personality, his work, and its influence will have taken a long step toward an understanding of the twentieth century."[1] Einstein ushered in a new view of the world. His influence extends through the whole field of science and into the arts and the broader culture.

1 Childhood: 1879-1895

On March 14, 1879, Albert Einstein was born in Ulm, Germany, the first child of Hermann and Pauline Einstein. Ulm, a small village built on the banks of the Danube River, lies in the foothills of the Swabian Alps. By nature, the Swabians are a gentle, creative, and joyful people, whose qualities are reflected in their flowing, melodic speech. Here in Swabia, Einstein's Jewish ancestors had lived for many generations as merchants, shopkeepers, and artisans. Einstein's father had set up a small electrical and engineering shop in Ulm a few years before Einstein was born.

Einstein's parents were a devoted couple who enjoyed their lives and their families. A friendly, easy-going man, Hermann Einstein took neither the Jewish religion nor his business very seriously. Although he enjoyed reading German philosophy, he had no notable intellectual achievements. Einstein's mother Pauline came from a family of grain merchants, somewhat wealthier than the Einstein family. She brought music and art into the family and played Beethoven's sonatas and read German literature. A more serious, better organized, and more ambitious person

Hermann and Pauline Einstein, parents of the famous physicist, lived in German Swabia when Albert was born in 1879.

The earliest known photograph of Einstein, probably taken in Munich where his family moved when he was a year old.

Maja. After a few years, the Einsteins moved their families and their business to the suburb of Sendling. There they lived in adjoining houses with a large shared garden.

The large garden was the children's playground. As an adult Maja remembered running and jumping with groups of children and playing soldier. She also recalled that her brother never liked rough, active play. Rather, he was a daydreamer who liked games that took patience; he built complicated structures with blocks and made houses of cards fourteen stories high. In spite of their different interests, brother and sister were good friends. Biographer Ronald Clark said that Maja became Einstein's "constant companion and unfailing confidant."[2]

Albert and his sister Maja, although different, were very close friends as they grew up.

than her husband, she was the parent who later emphasized her children's education. Though Einstein lived in Ulm only a year, his Swabian origin had a lifelong influence on him, and he still spoke the melodic Swabian dialect in his old age.

When Einstein was a year old, his family moved to Munich, Germany, where Hermann and his brother Jakob set up a small electrochemical factory. In the new factory, Einstein's father managed the business, and his uncle did the engineering work. In Munich, a large city, the Einstein family often missed the countryside of their native Ulm. To get away from the big city, Einstein's father Hermann took his family on frequent outings in the beautiful mountains around Munich. When Albert was two, the Einsteins had a second child,

Einstein was a humble and modest man. An excerpt from Phillip Frank's book Einstein: His Life and Times *tells of humbling childhood experiences that may have influenced Einstein's attitude:*

"Even when Albert was nine years old and in the highest grade of the elementary school, he still lacked fluency of speech, and everything he said was expressed only after thorough consideration and reflection. Because of his conscientiousness in not making any false statements or telling lies he was called *Biedermeier* (Honest John) by his classmates. He was regarded as an amiable dreamer. As yet no evidence of any special talent could be discovered, and his mother remarked occasionally: 'Maybe he will become a great professor some day.' But perhaps she meant only that he might develop into some sort of eccentric."

An Unusual Child

Early in his life, Einstein's parents worried that he was developmentally slow. As a young child Albert was slow to talk. In a letter written in 1954, Einstein looked back on this period: "My parents were worried because I started to talk comparatively late, and they consulted the doctor because of it. I cannot tell you how old I was at the time, but certainly not younger than three."[3] The delay in his speech affected him later in his life. As a school-age boy, he could be seen repeating words and sentences to himself in order to avoid mistakes when he spoke. As an adult, he still lacked confidence and joked that he would never become an orator.

Einstein was an imaginative and creative child. From an early age, he was curious about why things happened, about what was hidden behind what he saw.

When Einstein at age five was home, sick in bed, his father brought a pocket compass for him. Einstein played with it a long time, turning it around and around and watching the needle which always pointed north. This discovery made a vivid impression on him. He recalled the incident many years later:

> That this needle behaved in such a determined way did not at all fit into the kind of occurrences that could find a place in the unconscious world of concepts. . . . I can still remember—or at least believe I can remember—that this experience made a deep and lasting impression upon me. Something deeply hidden had to be behind things.[4]

Einstein referred to this experience as the first "wonder" of his childhood. Even at five his imagination sensed big and abstract ideas.

A drawing depicts the nineteenth-century German emperor reviewing his troops on parade. After viewing a similar military parade with his family, young Einstein expressed disgust regarding military authority and regimentation.

Even as a child, Einstein could be stubborn and often rebelled against authority. One example of his early dislike of following authority came when the family was watching a military parade. As the soldiers marched through the streets with drums beating and fifes playing, many parents told their children that they would grow big and could then march in parades too. But Einstein cried and said, "When I grow up I don't want to be one of those poor people."[5] This child intuitively disliked soldiers and later explained that he thought the men were coerced into being soldiers, and the parade forced them to act like a machine. This early experience stayed with him, and he always hated any kind of military authority. He also hated other types of authority, an attitude that became more pronounced as he entered school.

A Jewish Boy in a Catholic School

At age six Einstein began violin lessons and started school. He took violin lessons for seven years because his parents insisted, but he disliked his teacher who made him memorize musical techniques by rote. He fared a bit better in school. Because the Jewish school was far from their house, the Einsteins sent Albert to the neighborhood Catholic school where he was the only Jewish child. There he learned the traditions and beliefs of the Catholic faith, as well as stories from the Bible. He especially liked the stories and learned about Catholicism so well that he helped his classmates on quizzes. In 1886—Einstein was seven at the time—his

Hard Lessons for a Sensitive Young Boy

In 1930 Einstein's son-in-law Rudolf Kayser published a biography, one of the few that Einstein endorsed, under the pseudonym Anton Reiser. In this biography entitled Albert Einstein: A Biographical Portrait, *the author describes the emotional difficulties young Albert faced in his first school years:*

"Albert Einstein, shy and slow, entered school at the age of six; first, primary school, since the Prussian system of combined elementary and secondary schools was unknown in Bavaria. From the lowest to the highest grade, school was ever to him a burdensome duty.

The methods of instruction in the primary school were far removed from any educational ideal. Rules were enforced mechanically with the ample support of thrashings and harsh words. The reigning atmosphere was hard and brutal.

In the large, overflowing classes the difference between the children of rich and poor parents was marked. In contrast to the poor, the rich children seemed strangely to show a greater power of holding out against the brutality of the school. For them after a few hours everything was over; the small pupils were again the spoiled darlings of rich citizens in Munich. For the poor children, however, there was no escape; they returned from school to the gloom and lovelessness of poverty.

Young Albert Einstein thus experienced the social problem for the first time. He never forgot his first glimpse of the injustice which prevails in human society.

At school, his religious instruction was Catholic; at home, Jewish. But he did not feel religious differences. On the contrary, he perceived the sameness of all religions. The stories of the Old Testament and Jesus' Way of Sorrow impressed him with equal power.

The Catholic teacher of religion liked him. But one day the same teacher brought a large nail to class and told the pupils that it was a nail with which the Jews had nailed Jesus to the cross. The incident stimulated in the pupils anti-Semitic feeling which was turned against their fellow-student Einstein. For the first time Albert experienced the frightful venom of anti-Semitism."

mother wrote to his grandmother, Jette Koch, "Yesterday Albert got his school marks. Again he is at the top of his class and got a brilliant record."[6] Although Einstein did well in school during the first few years, his enthusiasm lasted only a short time before he resisted rote learning and authoritarian rules. When he left elementary school, he compared it to a military barracks where teachers emphasized obedience and made children stand at attention whenever teachers spoke to them.

Although Einstein disliked the rigidity of school, he took great pleasure in informal lessons. His uncle Jakob, a trained engineer who was more intellectual than his father, used stories to introduce Einstein to algebra. He told Einstein, "Algebra is a merry science. We go hunting for a little animal whose name we don't know, so we call it *x*. When we bag our game we pounce on it and give it its right name."[7] His uncle Jakob also told him about a theorem for a triangle; then, on his own Einstein found a way to prove the theorem. He liked these problems because they piqued his imagination and satisfied his love of logical reasoning.

Informal Lessons and Private Study

At age ten Einstein entered Luitpold Gymnasium—a high school that taught a classical education, which includes such subjects as mathematics, science, literature, Greek and Latin grammar, and culture. At this school Einstein disliked the even greater emphasis on obedience and rote instruction and took refuge in informal study. At twelve he found a school mathematics book which taught Euclidean plane geometry, and he began reading it on his own. He worked his way through the whole book, making notes in the margin and solving problems. The book appealed

A painting of a nineteenth-century German primary school such as Einstein attended. Although Albert did well in school, he soon tired of the rote learning and emphasis on obedience.

Probl I

Investiganda est curva Linea ADB in qua grave a dato quovis puncto A ad datum quodvis punctum B vi gravitatis suæ citissimè descendet

Solutio.

A dato puncto A ducatur recta infinita APCZ horizonti parallela et super eadem recta describatur tum Cyclois quæcunq; AQP rectæ AB (ducta et si opus est producta) occurrens in puncto Q, tum Cyclois alia ADC cujus basis et altitudo sit ad prioris basem et altitudinem respectivè ut AB ad AQ. Et hæc Cyclois novissima transibit per punctum B et erit Curva illa linea in qua grave a puncto A ad punctum B vi gravitatis suæ citissimè perveniet. Q.E.J.

This solution, in Latin, to the difficult geometry problem, was written by Sir Isaac Newton, the English physicist. Einstein would later prove many of Newton's laws to be inaccurate.

to him because he could think step by step until he arrived at an answer. Like the compass, geometry made a lasting impression on him. Later he wrote,

> At the age of 12—I experienced a second wonder of a totally different nature. . . . Here were assertions, as for example the intersection of the three altitudes of a triangle at one point, which . . . could nevertheless be proved with such certainty that any doubt appeared to be out of the question; [however] this "wonder" rested upon an error. Nevertheless, for anyone who experiences it for the first time, it is marvellous enough that man is capable at all to reach such a degree and purity in pure thinking as the Greeks showed us for the first time to be possible in geometry.[8]

Einstein was interested in geometry for two reasons: first, the problems had definite and sure answers and, second, he could arrive at answers by thinking.

Broadening Horizons

During these preteenage years Einstein's informal lessons and private study became increasingly important to him and to his academic and personal development. After learning the pleasure of studying mathematics, he found new pleasure in reading science and philosophy. Max Talmey, a medical student and family friend who came to dinner every Thursday, gave Einstein five or six volumes of Aaron Bernstein's *Popular Books on Natural Science.* These books told about animals and plants and their mutual interdependence, about stars, meteors, volcanoes, earthquakes, climate, and the whole inter-relationship of nature. In school, Einstein had been taught to see the world as a collection of disconnected rules and demands, whereas these books showed him an orderly and interconnected world of nature. When Talmey saw that Einstein read the science books with "breathless attention," he gave him a book by a philosopher, Immanuel Kant. Talmey said later, "I recommended to him the reading of Kant. At that time he was still a child, only thirteen years old, yet Kant's works, incomprehensible to ordinary mortals, seemed clear to him."[9] This interest in philosophy acquired at thirteen became a lifelong interest. Little by little in his reading and studying, Einstein developed a way of understanding the world as a whole and a way of thinking, or reasoning, about it.

Religious Experiences

While Einstein's childhood experiences with mathematics, science, and philosophy would affect his future scientific work, his childhood religious experiences profoundly affected his view of the universe, which, in turn, affected his scientific work. Einstein's early enthusiasm for Catholicism gave way to an interest in his parents' faith, Judaism.

The Einsteins were nonpracticing Jews. They did not follow any of the Jewish traditions concerning food, nor did they attend synagogue. Hermann Einstein thought such things were ancient superstitions, and he made his feelings known to the family. Since he knew little of his own religion, Einstein took a course in Judaism available at the gymnasium. In this course

he was particularly impressed with the study of the Old Testament and the wisdom of Solomon. For the first time he learned about Jewish traditions concerning food and holidays. He made up his mind to become religious, both in spirit and in practice. He disapproved of his parents' apathy toward religion. He refused to eat pork and followed Jewish practices by himself. Just as geometry's certainty appealed to him, so did the certainty of religious traditions. Einstein later explained that the religious intensity he experienced when he was ten or eleven gave him security. He called it "the religious paradise of youth."[10]

But Einstein's interest slowly gave way to rejection of these beliefs. After reading science books, he concluded that the Bible stories he had learned in the two

Famed eighteenth-century German philosopher Immanuel Kant's writings introduced Einstein to philosophy at the tender age of thirteen.

Einstein's Concept of God

Einstein understood the goal of religion and the goal of science to be one and the same. Thus, the word "God" appears often in Einstein's writings. In Einstein: The Life and Times, *Ronald W. Clark tells what he thinks Einstein meant by the word "God" and how the definition relates to Einstein's work:*

"But much of Einstein's writing gives the impression of belief in a God even more intangible and impersonal than a celestial machine minder, running the universe with undisputable authority and expert touch. Instead, Einstein's God appears as the physical world itself, with its infinitely marvelous structure operating at atomic level with the beauty of a craftsman's wristwatch, and at stellar level with the majesty of a massive cyclotron. This was belief enough. It grew early and rooted deep. Only later was it dignified by the title of cosmic religion, a phrase which gave plausible respectability to the views of a man who did not believe in a life after death and who felt that if virtue paid off in the earthly one, then this was the result of cause and effect rather than celestial reward. Einstein's God thus stood for an orderly system obeying rules which could be discovered by those who had the courage, imagination, and the persistence to go on searching for them. And it was to this task which he began to turn his mind soon after the age of twelve. For the rest of his life everything else was to seem almost trivial by comparison."

schools could not be literally true because they did not fit the world of nature. His own reasoning and his suspicious attitude about authoritarian teaching clinched these doubts. He reasoned that authorities taught religion to all people in a machine-like way to make them feel that life is less cruel than it really is and to give them hope. He concluded that by teaching religion, schools taught children lies. Einstein grew to mistrust every kind of authority; he became suspicious of all society. This skeptical attitude never left him.

Studying the Universe

After rejecting his religious training, Einstein took solace in science and math. Security and order could be found in the natural order of the universe, which Einstein saw as dependable, even if it was not as comforting as religion. It was a universe with rules and laws he could learn. Individuals he admired had studied this universe, and Einstein decided that he would study it, too. With that decision Einstein

The logical order of the universe gave the young Einstein a greater sense of security than did the tenets of religion.

beckoned as a liberation, and I soon noticed that many a man whom I had learned to esteem and to admire had found inner freedom and security in its pursuit. The mental grasp of this extra-personal world within the frame of our capacities presented itself to my mind, half consciously, half unconsciously, as a supreme goal. Similarly motivated men of the present and of the past, as well as the insights they had achieved, were the friends who could not be lost. The road to this paradise was not as comfortable and alluring as the road to religious paradise; but it has shown itself reliable, and I have never regretted having chosen it.[11]

Einstein's Teen Years and the Gymnasium

Einstein's resistance to authority and his independence continued to determine his private study and affect his school courses. He studied the principles of differential and integral calculus which he enjoyed as much as geometry, both for their certainty and their reasoned order. His success in mathematics at this time was helpful to him later on when he needed a good recommendation from a teacher.

Einstein, however, developed a poor reputation with most of the teachers at the gymnasium. He had the most trouble with the teacher of Greek. Einstein had a poor memory for words and texts. His poor memory was aggravated by his resistance to methodical rote learning. He chose to endure the teacher's punishments rather than obey the teacher's rules. In frustration his Greek teacher told him, "You will never amount to anything."[12] Others at

set his life goal, one that he worked on until the day he died. Later on he reflected upon his decision this way:

> Out yonder there was this huge world, which exists independent of us human beings and which stands before us like a great, eternal riddle, at least partially accessible to our inspection and thinking. The contemplation of this world

Freedom to Explore

When Einstein was fifteen, he risked his future and left the gymnasium. The doctor's certificate and his mathematics teacher's letter were his security. The next few months in Milan gave him the freedom and joy that he longed for. Banesh Hoffmann describes Einstein's move to Milan in his biography Albert Einstein: Creator and Rebel:

"Armed with these documents, Albert threw further caution to the winds. The future would have to take care of itself. After all, he could prepare himself by self study for entrance to a university. Although the medical certificate troubled his conscience, it saved him from being branded a truant, but, to put it bluntly, he became a school dropout. Fleeing his bleak Munich existence, he rejoined his family in Milan, and what followed was one of the most joyous periods of his life. He allowed no ties of school or state to mar his new-found liberty. For better or worse, he roamed far and wide in mind and body, forsaking all cares—an independent spirit wedded to freedom, studying only the subjects he loved. With his friend Otto Neustätter he hiked fancy-free through the Apennine mountains to Genoa, where he had relatives. Museums, art treasures, churches, concerts, books and more books, family, friends, the warm Italian sun, the free, warmhearted people—all merged into a heady adventure of escape and wonderful self-discovery."

the school shared the teacher's opinion. When Hermann Einstein asked the headmaster what profession he should encourage his son to go into, the headmaster told him that it did not matter because Albert would never make a success of anything. In short, Einstein was hardly a model student, and the school clearly disliked his attitude.

As Einstein neared the end of his studies at Luitpold Gymnasium, the family business came upon hard times. In 1894 the brothers gave up the factory and moved to Milan, Italy. Since Einstein had only one year left until graduation, he stayed behind to finish. Watched over by a distant relative, he lived alone in a single room. Einstein missed his family, hated his life in Munich, and longed to move to Milan. Feeling depressed, he asked his father for help. His father helped him obtain a medical certificate saying that his depression required him to return to his family. The school offered no resistance and even encouraged him to leave. The homeroom teacher summed up the school's attitude toward Einstein: "Your mere presence spoils the respect of the class for me."[13] Einstein withdrew from the gymnasium and moved to Milan; he became a high school dropout.

With his move to Milan, he asked his

A portrait of the twelve-year-old Einstein. At this age he discovered the wonders of mathematics, philosophy, and natural science that would thereafter so deeply affect his life.

father to help him give up his German citizenship; by this time he had become bitter about German authoritarian ways and German schools and wanted to sever all ties with Germany. Later on, he officially renounced his citizenship. At fifteen, Einstein was without a school, without a religion, and without a country. He planned to have time off from school, live in Milan, and then take the university entrance exams. In the meantime he enjoyed his family, the Italian countryside, Italian culture, and freedom. The escape from Germany, the pleasures of Italy, and the prospect of entering the university gave Einstein a feeling of optimism, but his plans to continue his education and fulfill his goal in science turned out to be more difficult than he had expected.

2 University Education and Career Plans: 1895-1905

While Einstein enjoyed the Italian countryside, its people and its culture, his father's business again failed. Hermann Einstein said he could no longer support his son and urged him to prepare for a practical profession and think about his future. In the fall of 1895 when he was still sixteen, Einstein took the university entrance exams at the Swiss Federal Polytechnic School, exams intended for students who were eighteen years old. He scored well in physics and mathematics, but failed the exams in languages, zoology, and botany. He was disappointed, but Albin Herzog, the director of Polytechnic, was impressed with Einstein's mathematical ability and urged Einstein to get a diploma from the Swiss Cantonal School of Aargua in Aarau so that he could enter the university the following year. After his bitter experiences at the Luitpold Gymnasium, Einstein was reluctant to go to Aarau. But to his surprise he found the school to be pleasantly different from Luitpold, and he thrived.

School in Aarau

In Aarau Einstein was happy and academically successful. He lived with Jost Winteler, a teacher at the school who treated Einstein as one of his family. Winteler had one son, who later married Einstein's sister Maja. Unlike the Munich gymnasium, Aarau had an atmosphere of freedom, and teachers discussed schoolwork with students in friendly conversations and encouraged them to think independently. Einstein felt at home and made friends, in

Einstein during his time at the Swiss Cantonal School of Aargua at Aarau.

Einstein's Kind of School

Biographer Phillip Frank, in Einstein: His Life and Times, *describes the school in Aarau, giving the details that changed Einstein's attitude about school:*

"Einstein went to Aarau with considerable misgiving and apprehension, but he was pleasantly surprised. The cantonal school was conducted in a very different spirit from that of the Munich gymnasium. There was no militaristic drilling, and the teaching was aimed at training the students to think and work independently. The teachers were always available to the students for friendly discussions or counsel. The students were not required to remain in the same room all the time, and there were separate rooms containing instruments, specimens, and accessories for every subject. For physics and chemistry there were apparatuses with which students could experiment. For zoology there were a small museum and microscopes for observing minute organisms, and for geography there were maps and pictures of foreign countries.

Here Einstein lost his aversion to school. He became more friendly with his fellow students. . . . He also had an opportunity to discuss problems of public life in detail with people who, in accordance with the Swiss tradition, were greatly interested in such affairs. He became acquainted with a point of view different from that which he had been accustomed to in Germany."

particular a fellow music student named Byland. Einstein's science classes were challenging, but he continued to read on his own.

Questions About Light

Einstein studied the theory of light developed by Scottish physicist James Clerk Maxwell, who concluded that light is a wave, the theory accepted by scientists at the time. Einstein thought about light beams and their speed. He came up with the question: What would a light beam look like if a person could travel alongside it at the same speed? Einstein wondered: To the person traveling at the same speed, would the light beam appear to be standing still? With this question, Einstein began to realize that a moving object may appear to move at different speeds depending on where the person is when viewing it. In *The Cosmic Code* Heinz R. Pagels explained what Einstein's speculation about light meant:

> If you could catch up to one of Maxwell's light waves the way a surfboarder catches an ocean wave for a ride, then the light wave would not be moving relative to you but instead be standing still. The light wave would then be a standing wave of electric and magnetic fields that is not allowed if Maxwell's theory is right. So, he [Einstein] reasoned, there must be something wrong with the assumption that you can catch a light wave as you can catch a water wave. This idea was the seed from which the special theory of relativity grew nine years later. Accord-

ing to that theory, no material object can attain the speed of light. It is the speed limit for the universe.[14]

Einstein did not find an answer to his light-beam question at the time, but more important than an answer was Einstein's ability to ask such a relevant question at sixteen. The question indicates his knowledge of physics and his ability to get to the heart of a problem by reasoning.

Entrance to the University

At the end of his inspiring year in Aarau, Einstein had earned a diploma and had decided to prepare for a career in teaching instead of engineering, the career his father had suggested. During the summer of 1896, Einstein passed the Zurich Polytechnic entrance exams and in October began studies to become a mathematics and science teacher. While at the university he took courses in mathematics, physics, astrophysics, astronomy, anthropology, and geology to prepare for teaching. He also took courses in business, politics, literature, and philosophy because the subjects interested him. His favorite subject was still physics, and he spent many hours in the laboratory working on research.

Scottish physicist James Clerk Maxwell theorized that light traveled in waves. Einstein's study of Maxwell's theory later led to his own theories of relativity.

Years at the University

Because of his father's business failures, Einstein lived in poverty during his university years. He lived in a modest room in the suburb of Hottingen and ate at restaurants for poor people, like soup kitchens. Fortunately, his mother's relatives in

Genoa gave him a monthly allowance of one hundred francs. Each month he saved twenty francs so that he could eventually pay the fees for a Swiss citizenship. On the remaining eighty francs he could afford few pleasures and little social life. He entertained himself by playing his violin and attending free musical performances. He had a small circle of friends with whom he shared serious conversation and humor, friends he had met at the university: Marcel Grossman, Mileva Maric, and Michele Besso. His friends considered him an eccentric because he wore unconventional clothes and cared little for social manners.

At the university his childhood habits of resisting class instruction returned. He was disappointed in some of his science courses because they failed to include the most important new information in science, and the lectures were poorly presented. Consequently, he began to cut

Einstein: The Eccentric

Early on, Einstein developed a strong will and a vehement disregard for social conventions. In a paper entitled "Einstein," excerpted from Einstein: The First Hundred Years, *C. P. Snow reflects on Einstein's years as a young man in Zurich and Bern and how they demonstrated Einstein's nonconformity:*

"Yes, no one has been less conventional. . . . Free-and-easy people take the conventions more lightly, sometimes dropping them, sometimes drifting along. It's more convenient, I should have thought, to get into a dinner jacket than to hack away at shirt-sleeves with a razor in order to make a kind of under-vest: but Einstein would firmly have thought the opposite. About him, even in Jehovianic old age, there was still a residue . . . of a non-conformer from a central European cafe . . . who made an impact by wearing odd shoes and his coat on backwards.

As a very young man, when he was producing great discoveries, Einstein's only society was in just those cafes. He was the least gregarious of humankind—he spoke of his own 'unconcealed lack of the need to frequent my fellow human beings and human communities'. Yet he enjoyed the desultory easy-going European nights, the cigars, the coffee, the talk; he was both witty and merry, he had a reverberating laugh, he didn't give a damn. When life had sobered him, when he felt responsibility for so much, he missed those nights. . . . So far as he was ever at home, at any time in his life, it was in Bern and Zurich before the First World War."

classes. He antagonized his physics professor by calling him "Herr Weber" when students properly called him "Herr Professor." As a result of his behavior, the professors were satisfied neither with his attitude nor with his work and informed him that he would not graduate. But Einstein continued his habit of intense private study. As Anton Reiser said of these years: "With a veritable mania for reading, day and night, he went through the works of the great physicists—Kirchhoff, Hertz, Helmholtz, Foppel." He read "everything of value to a knowledge of nature and the human spirit."[15]

Struggling to Pass Exams

Furthermore, Einstein hated exams because they forced him to be tested on material he thought less important than what he studied on his own. To graduate, Einstein had to prepare for and pass two major exams that covered what he had learned in his courses during the entire four years. Because of his irregular attendance at lectures, Einstein was poorly prepared to take his exams. Fortunately, his friend Marcel Grossman helped him. Grossman had attended every lecture and taken careful notes. He recognized Einstein's talent and allowed him to study these notes. Consequently, Einstein passed his exams and graduated in August 1900, with an average score of 4.9 out of a possible 6.0. He had not made an outstanding record, but he had earned a degree.

It was the custom for students with degrees from Polytechnic to receive offers for low-level assistantships from their former professors. Unfortunately, Einstein's

major interest was physics, and Heinrich Weber, whom Einstein had addressed inappropriately, was the physics professor. He told Einstein, "You're a clever fellow! But you have one fault. You won't let anyone tell you a thing."[16] Weber overlooked Einstein, he got no offer, and both his pride and his job prospects suffered as a result. In *Einstein: The Life and Times*, Ronald W. Clark explained the effects of Einstein's independence:

> In the autumn of 1900 Albert Einstein was the graduate who denied rather than defied authority, the perverse young man for whom "you must" was the father of "I won't," the keen seeker out of heresies to support; a young man who was written off as virtually unemployable by many self-respecting citizens.
>
> These awkward facts became apparent throughout the next few months. One of the first results of Einstein's failure to gain a post in the ETH [Polytechnic] was the summary ending of his allowance from the Koch relations in Genoa. . . . He crossed the Alps once more to join his parents in Milan, and from here, in September, 1900, wrote the first of numerous letters asking for work.[17]

Search for Jobs

During the fall of 1900 and spring of 1901, Einstein applied to two of his former Polytechnic professors, Adolf Hurwitz in mathematics and Alfred Wolfer in astrophysics and astronomy. Hurwitz offered Einstein nothing, and Wolfer offered him only a temporary task. Meanwhile, Einstein continued his scientific study and wrote papers on the nature of atoms and the nature of energy. He wrote a paper on capillarity, which concerns the interaction between a liquid and the solid surface of its container. Einstein's paper was about the question of how and why atoms combine with other atoms in capillarity. In December 1900, he sent the paper to *Annalen der Physik*, a scholarly journal, which published it the next year. In the spring of 1901, Einstein wrote a paper on thermodynamics, which was about the relationships between heat and other forms of energy. This paper suggested a new method to investigate the molecular forces that occur in these relationships. The *Annalen der Physik* published the paper in April 1902.

Wilhelm Ostwald, a University of Leipzig physics professor and later Nobel Prize winner, refused to give Einstein a teaching job at the university in 1901.

Having papers published in this scholarly journal indicated that Einstein's work was worthy of serious, scholarly consideration.

Einstein also submitted these papers to universities, hoping they would help him obtain a teaching job or an advanced degree. On March 19, 1901, Einstein sent his paper on capillarity to Professor Wilhelm Ostwald (later a Nobel Prize winner) at the University of Leipzig, Germany, and requested a position as a mathematical physicist. He followed up with a postcard on April 4, and unknown to Einstein, his father also wrote to Professor Ostwald on April 17, pleading that his son be given a job. Nothing came of these requests. Einstein tried again to get an assistantship by writing to Professor Heike Kamerlingh-Onner of the University of Leiden, Netherlands, again sending a copy of his paper on capillarity and this time sending a self-addressed, stamped card for a reply. Einstein again heard nothing, and his blank card appeared years later among the professor's papers. Einstein tried another angle by submitting his paper on thermodynamics to the University of Zurich in application for a doctoral degree, thinking his chances for a teaching position would be enhanced if he had an advanced degree. But the university denied his request.

Application for Swiss Citizenship

Einstein became depressed in these months. He "felt himself sinking helplessly in the quagmire of a world that had no place for him."[18] Biographer Anton Reiser suggested that Einstein's troubles may

A Father's Plea for His Son

Shortly before he died, Hermann Einstein wrote a letter on his son's behalf to Professor Ostwald, the Leipzig professor Einstein hoped would offer him a job as a mathematical physicist. The letter, revealing a father's love and concern for his son, appears in Banesh Hoffmann's biography Albert Einstein: Creator and Rebel:

"I beg you to excuse a father who dares to approach you, dear Professor, in the interests of his son.

I wish to mention first that my son Albert Einstein is 22 years old, has studied for four years at the Zurich Polytechnic and last summer brilliantly passed his diploma examinations in mathematics and physics. Since then he has tried unsuccessfully to find a position as assistant, which would enable him to continue his education in theoretical and experimental physics. Everybody who is able to judge praises his talent, and in any case I can assure you that he is exceedingly assiduous and industrious and is attached to his science with a great love.

My son is profoundly unhappy about his present joblessness, and every day the idea becomes more firmly implanted in him that he is a failure in his career and will not be able to find the way back again. And on top of this he is depressed by the thought that he is a burden on us since we are not very well-to-do people.

Because, dear Professor, my son honors and reveres you the most among all the great physicists of our time, I permit myself to apply to you with the plea that you will read his article published in the *Annalen der Physik* and, hopefully, that you will write him a few lines of encouragement so that he may regain his joy in his life and his work.

If, in addition, it should be possible for you to obtain for him a position as assistant, now or in the fall, my gratitude would be boundless.

I beg again your forgiveness for my audacity in sending you this letter and I want to add that my son has no idea of this extraordinary step of mine."

have been aggravated because he was a Jew and not a citizen of any country. In the fall of 1900, Einstein had saved enough money and applied for Swiss citizenship, but even that application had problems. In *Albert Einstein: A Biographical Portrait*, Anton Reiser described Einstein's examination:

The Zurich city fathers definitely mistrusted the unworldly, dreamy young scholar of German descent who was so bound to become a citizen of Switzerland. They could not be too sure that he was not engaged in dangerous practices. They decided to examine the young man in person and to question him rigorously. Was he inclined to drink, had his grandfather been syphilitic, did he himself lead a proper life? Young Einstein had to give information on all these questions. He had hardly suspected that the acquisition of Swiss naturalization papers was so morally involved a matter. Finally the high authorities observed how harmless and how innocent of the world the young man was. They laughed at him, teased him about his ignorance of the world and finally honored him by recognizing his right to Swiss citizenship.[19]

On February 21, 1901, after five years as a person with no citizenship, he was now a Swiss citizen.

A Job at Last

Gradually, Einstein's fortune changed as he was hired for a series of temporary jobs. Between May and July 1901, he substituted for a mathematics teacher at the school he had attended in Aarau. Then he acquired another substitute teaching job at Technical School in Wintherthur, Switzerland. Next, he was hired for a few months to tutor an English boy. After these temporary jobs, Einstein received help from his friend Marcel Grossman, who had asked his father to use his influence with Friedrich Haller, the director of the Swiss Patent Office in Bern, Switzerland. After a long interview, Haller offered Einstein a position as a clerk to analyze requests for patents as soon as there was an opening. The vacancy occurred in December, 1901. Einstein moved to Bern in February and began work at the Patent Office on June 23, 1902. At twenty-three Einstein had his first full-time job.

Besides the optimism that came with full-time employment, Einstein's move to Bern brought changes in his personal and family life. First, he made several close friends. While waiting for the Patent Office job to begin, Einstein tutored a Rumanian student named Maurice Solovine, who wanted to learn about physics. The meeting began a lifelong friendship for discussion of scientific ideas. Their regular

Einstein at his first full-time job at the Swiss Patent Office in Bern.

Thanks to a Friend for Help

Marcel Grossman asked his father to help Einstein get a job at the Patent Office in Bern. Thanking his friend, Einstein wrote the following letter, printed in Banesh Hoffman's biography Albert Einstein: Creator and Rebel:

"Dear Marcel,

When I found your letter yesterday I was deeply moved by your devotion and compassion which do not let you forget an old, unlucky friend. . . . Needless to say, I would be delighted to get the job. I would spare no effort to live up to your recommendation. I have spent three weeks at my parents' home looking for a position of assistant lecturer at some university. I am sure I would have found one long ago were it not for Weber's intrigues against me. In spite of all this, I don't let a single opportunity pass unheeded, nor have I lost my sense of humor. . . . When God created the ass he gave him a thick skin."

meetings soon included Einstein's friend Konrad Habicht, a mathematics scholar, and evolved into the "Olympia Academy," jokingly named after Mount Olympus, the home of the Greek gods. They met for simple dinners and long conversations about physics, philosophy, and literature and some fun and wit. Einstein explained later that these conversations influenced his ideas.

Unfortunately, in the midst of these positive changes, Einstein's father died on October 10, 1902. Einstein felt shattered and desolate with the loss of his father and said he should have died instead. Shortly after his father's death, Einstein married his university friend Mileva Maric on January 6, 1903. Maric was a Serbian woman who had studied physics at the Polytechnic and was part of the small group that gathered around Einstein for conversation. While at the university, she and Ein-

Albert and Mileva Einstein shortly after their marriage.

(Left) The "Olympia Academy" founders (left to right) Konrad Habicht, Maurice Solovine, and Albert Einstein. (Below) Mileva and Albert with their firstborn, Hans.

stein spent many hours sailing on the lakes near Zurich and discussing physics in the cafés in the city. Though she and Einstein were compatible student friends, they were less compatible as husband and wife. In 1904 a son Hans Albert was born. In spite of imperfections, Einstein's life was more stable than it had been for many years. The job was a blessing: he admired his boss, he was financially independent of his relatives, and he had the security of friends and his family, even though he missed his own father.

Unexpectedly the patent job helped Einstein in his work as a physicist. Quick to analyze the applications for patents, Einstein learned his clerk job easily. He used the spare time to think about his scientific ideas and work on equations. Feeling guilty, he listened for footsteps and hid his equations in a drawer to avoid detection. Yet the spare time produced results. Between 1902 and 1904 he wrote three new papers on thermodynamics, all

Einstein's Need for Freedom

Einstein hated the confinement of class lectures and course exams. In his Autobiographical Notes, *he compares forcing students to learn to forcing animals to eat:*

"It is, in fact, nothing short of a miracle that the modern methods of instruction have not yet entirely strangled the holy curiosity of inquiry; for this delicate little plant, aside from stimulation, stands mainly in need of freedom; without this it goes to wrack and ruin without fail. It is a very grave mistake to think that the enjoyment of seeing and searching can be promoted by means of coercion and a sense of duty. To the contrary, I believe that it would be possible to rob even a healthy beast of prey of its voraciousness, if it were possible, with the aid of a whip, to force the beast to devour continuously, even when not hungry, especially if the food, handed out under coercion, were to be selected accordingly."

of which *Annalen der Physik* published. Einstein used these papers and the two he had written previously to examine ways to prove abstract theories and to see which type of scientific problems were of interest to him.

Although Einstein now had enough quiet time to think, he lacked a good library and access to new publications in science. The "Olympia Academy" broke up when Habicht moved to Schaffhausen, Switzerland, and Solovine moved to Paris, France. Einstein was without stimulating conversation and the publications these two men made available. He then called on his university friend Michele Besso, who was now an engineer, and urged him to take a job at the Patent Office. He did, and Einstein found in Besso a friend who listened to his scientific ideas and theories and understood, questioned, and criticized them. These conversations helped

Einstein to refine his ideas.

The events during the ten-year period leading up to 1905 profoundly affected both Einstein's personality and his career. The disappointments and failures he encountered in attempting to find a job reinforced his shyness and established a humility that marked a lifelong attitude about himself in spite of the fame he eventually achieved. Though his childhood experiences with mathematics, science, and religion gave him a vision and a goal, his private reading, the papers he wrote, the conversations with fellow scholars, and the quiet thought in the Patent Office contributed to the specific development of his ideas. Without knowing it, Einstein was about to enter a year of creative work that would leave scientists wondering how this unknown clerk in a patent office could produce five new scientific theories in a year's time. The year was 1905.

3 The 1905 Papers and Success: 1905-1914

Even though Einstein's life improved considerably when he began work as a clerk at the Patent Office, he still lacked the facilities and conveniences usual to those who work as theoretical physicists. Nevertheless, he pursued his goal as a scientist; he achieved a doctoral degree from the University of Zurich and published five papers in the *Annalen der Physik* in one year, 1905. Unlike the previous papers he had published in this scholarly journal, four of these 1905 papers made major changes in scientific thought and opened the way for new directions in research. Enough scientists recognized the significance of these papers to recommend him to faculties at universities, and in the years following 1905, Einstein had offers to teach at several universities and to speak at important scientific conferences.

Conditions at Work and Home

Scholars who develop important theories usually work in reputable universities. They usually have salaries that allow them to live comfortably, colleagues with whom they discuss problems and solutions, and the benefit of libraries and laboratories.

Einstein in 1905, the year he changed the study of physics. Virtually unknown when he published his theories, he astounded the scientific world.

The Clockwork Universe

In The Cosmic Code: Quantum Physics as the Language of Nature, *Heinz R. Pagels explains the Newtonian world that had been accepted since the seventeenth century. Accustomed to this world view, many people found Einstein's new theories and new world view upsetting and revolutionary:*

"Twentieth-century physics grew out of the previous 'classical' physics inspired by the work of Isaac Newton in the late seventeenth century. Newton discovered the laws of motion and gravity and successfully applied them to descriptions of the detailed motion of the planets and the moon. In the century following Newton's discoveries, a new interpretation of the universe emerged: determinism. According to determinism, the universe may be viewed as a great clockwork set in motion by a divine hand at the beginning of time and then left undisturbed. From its largest to its smallest motions the entire material creation moves in a way that can be predicted by the laws of Newton. Nothing is left to chance. The future is as precisely determined by the past as is the forward movement of a clock. Although our humans minds could never in practice track the movement of all the parts of the great clockwork and thus know the future, we can imagine that an all-knowing mind of God can do this and see past and future time laid out like a mountain range.

This rigid determinism implied by Newton's laws promotes a sense of security about the place of humanity in the universe. All that happens—the tragedy and joy of human life—is already predetermined. The objective universe exists independently of the human will and purpose. Nothing we do can alter it. The wheels of the great world clock turn as indifferently to human life as the silent motion of the stars. In a sense, eternity has already happened."

Einstein's situation was different. He did not have fellow professors who also worked on important researches, but he had his friends, Habicht and Solovine for a time and Besso later, who helped him formulate his ideas. When his friends were not close by, he wrote letters and clarified his ideas by mail. Nor did he have a library; consequently, he arrived at conclusions himself, often not knowing that other scholars were interested in some of the same problems in physics. He had one advantage over professors in universities, however. Einstein could focus his whole attention on his research, without sharing his time with teaching and students. Most important of all, the job gave him the time and opportunity to think about physics.

Einstein's personal life, however, presented obstacles. He was still poor and had a family to care for. The Einsteins lived in a small, crowded flat without luxuries. Later on Einstein referred to this period as the oil-lamp period because he could afford neither gas light nor electricity, which were both more expensive than oil. When a friend visited one day, he found the door open to dry the freshly scrubbed floors, laundry hanging in the hallway, and Einstein holding his son in one hand while writing equations with the

Isaac Newton's mechanical model of the universe was the physicist's gospel for more than two hundred years until Albert Einstein came along. Just as Newton's theories had overturned the medieval worldview, so did Einstein's make Newton's viewpoint obsolete.

other. In addition to his economic problems, Einstein had an unhappy marriage. At times, in order to avoid conflict with Mileva, he wheeled his son in a carriage through the streets of Bern. Amid these conditions he completed his dissertation papers for his doctoral degree for the University of Zurich, making a total of six papers since his graduation. As Ronald W. Clark writes, "It was a good record for a failed teacher who had ended up in the Patent Office; it was surprisingly little for a man who was about to shake the scientific world."[20]

Disturbing the Newtonian World

The scientific world Einstein disturbed was the world established by Isaac Newton when he published his *Principia* in 1687. According to Newton, God created a perfectly ordered universe, so well designed that once created it could be left to run itself. Newton's concept of the universe became known as the clockwork universe because it ticked on like an intricate clock. According to this view, the universe is absolute, which means that its parts and its workings are unchanging and have certain measurements, for example, distances, time, and objects. Newton established three laws of motion and a law of gravity according to this clockwork universe. His laws of motion, he argued, could be used to measure all objects, moving and stationary, whether an apple or the moon. His law of gravity, he said, explained how the universe was held in order. According to the Newtonian view, no human mind could comprehend this divine creation to-

Einstein's Influence on the History of Physics

When trying to explain historical changes, people often ask the question, "Do people make history, or do events make people important?" Biographer Ronald W. Clark gives his opinion of Einstein's place in history in Einstein: The Life and Times:

"Einstein thus comes on to the scene as a student at a moment when physics was about to be revolutionized but when few students were encouraged to be revolutionaries. Without his own basically dissenting spirit he would have got nowhere. With it, the almost inevitable consequence was that he pushed along with his formal work just as much as he had to and found his real education elsewhere, in his own time. . . . Einstein would have developed his original mind whatever happened; but the conformity of Weber, the pervasive air of a science learned for examination rather than for probing into the natural world, speeded up the process."

---

tally, but humans could measure its parts using Newton's equations. Scientists and lay people had accepted Newton's view for two hundred years. In short, Newton is important because his view of the universe overturned the view accepted by scholars since medieval times, and he established a new view.

Einstein and Newton were similar in many ways. Both worked in solitude. Both produced major ideas in short, creative periods. Both overturned established views of the universe. Though many scientists have called Einstein's theories revolutionary, Einstein himself thought that he had merely adjusted what was wrong with Newton's and other scientists' theories and then built upon them. In an article published originally in the *London Times* in 1919, he said, "Let no one suppose, however, that the mighty work of Newton can really be superseded by this or any other

theory. His great and lucid ideas will retain their unique significance for all time as the foundation of our whole modern conceptual structure in the sphere of natural philosophy." [21] In his humble way Einstein downplayed the importance of the work he did as a young man of twenty-six. But Heinz Pagels saw Einstein's theories differently: "These papers began the physics revolution of the twentieth century. It would be decades before a new consensus on the nature of physical reality could be formed." [22] Einstein published five papers in 1905 explaining these theories.

The First Paper

On March 17, 1905, Einstein sent a paper to *Annalen der Physik*. The paper began with the idea that light is composed of

German physicist Max Planck was a contemporary of Einstein. Planck's studies with heat energy helped Einstein develop his own particle theory of light.

tiny particles that look like a wave because they move so quickly (like a movie, which is a series of individual frames that look like smooth motion when the film runs). Finally, Einstein provided the photoelectric formula with which an experimenter could test the theory.

Einstein's paper, known later simply as his "photoelectric paper," caused little stir among scientists. A few experimenters tried to test the photoelectric formula, but the experiments were difficult to conduct and the results were inconclusive. Then American experimenter Robert Millikan, a man who liked difficult challenges, took on the task of testing Einstein's theory. Intending to show conclusively that the theory would fail in experiment, Millikan

American physicist Robert Millikan tried for ten years to disprove Einstein's photoelectric theory. He finally proved the theory valid.

particles; then it provided the reasoning that made the idea true and ended with a method for verifying the theory. Einstein's paper built upon German physicist Max Planck's work on heat energy. Max Planck discovered a single amount of heat on a scale ranging from hot to cold. He called the amounts of heat on the scale quanta, from the Greek word meaning "how much." Further, he identified a number to use as a standard measure for heat, which he called constant h. Einstein also knew that Greek scientists thought light might be tiny particles, as did Newton. From the information from these various sources, Einstein reasoned that light, like heat, could be measured in amounts, in quanta. He also reasoned that light is composed of

Cornelius Lanczos reflects on the qualities that make Einstein's 1905 work great, qualities that make the theories simple and elegant. Lanczos describes the 1905 papers in a lecture entitled "The Greatness of Albert Einstein," published in Albert Einstein and the Cosmic World Order:

"These papers were written in a peculiar style, very characteristic of Einstein's manner of thinking. They did not contain a great deal of mathematical formalism. There was a great deal of text and little in the line of formal manipulations. In the end the startling conclusion was there, obtained apparently with the greatest of ease, and by a reasoning which could not be refuted. Outside sources were hardly ever quoted; it looked as if the author had arrived at his results practically unaided, as if he had conjured up the whole procedure out of thin air, by a wave of his magic wand. This made Einstein suspicious in the eyes of his colleagues. A man who writes so clearly and with so few technicalities cannot be taken too seriously. Something must be wrong with him. It is not proper that he should deduce important results so elegantly, apparently without laborious efforts, and without consulting the opinions of others. And thus it happened that the majority of physicists ignored his work, while a few first-class minds, particularly Planck, Rubens, Nernst, and von Laue, accepted this amazing fledgling as a full-grown member of their august community, in spite of the fact that he was much younger."

worked for ten years. At the end of his experimentation, he found that Einstein's theory was correct. Millikan published the results in 1916 and received a Nobel Prize for the work in 1928. From 1916 on, scientists accepted Einstein's theory of light; the light quantum—the one particle of light—was called a "photon." This first 1905 paper and the word "quantum" had important effects on twentieth-century physics. The theory helped to form the basis for studying the structure of atoms and gave the name "quantum theory" to a collection of theories concerning atomic and nuclear physics. This theory, the law of the photoelectric effect, earned Einstein a Nobel Prize in 1921.

The Second Paper

In April 1905, barely a month after he sent the paper on light, Einstein sent another paper to *Annalen der Physik*. Called "A Determination of the Sizes of Molecules," his second paper proved the existence of molecules, which are made up of atoms. This theory showed that the size of molecules could be measured by observing how molecules dispersed, or spread out, in a liquid. Einstein reasoned that sugar molecules added to water, for example, would disperse and increase its viscosity, or resistance to flow. Einstein envisioned the sugar molecules as small spheres. Then he developed equations to show how the molecules, or spheres, would diffuse, or spread out, and how they would increase the viscosity of the water. Next he brought together the findings from other scientists' conclusions: tables showing diffusion rates, tables showing viscosities of various solutions, and Max

Einstein's observations of common, everyday events, such as the way his pipe smoke dispersed in the air, helped him conclude that everything, even time, was relative.

Planck's way of measuring a quantum, or an amount, in a continuous range. The result was a theory showing how to measure molecules as they spread out in a liquid in order to determine their size. This theory provided an equation that could be tested.

Einstein sent this paper to University of Zurich professor Kleiner as a possible thesis for a doctoral degree. Professor Kleiner had already rejected a paper Einstein had submitted in 1901 for a doctoral degree, causing Einstein to write in a letter to his friend Besso, "I shall not become a Ph.D. . . . the whole comedy has become a bore to me."[23] Apparently in 1905 Einstein changed his mind and submitted his paper, only to have it rejected because it was too short. Einstein added one sentence, resubmitted it, Professor Kleiner accepted it, and Einstein had a Ph.D. degree.

The Third Paper

In May 1905, within a month after he had written his paper on sugar molecules, Einstein sent his third paper to *Annalen der Physik*. Since no scientists had yet proved the existence of atoms, Einstein was still trying to find a way. Later, he wrote about his purpose: "My main aim . . . was to find facts that would guarantee as far as possible the existence of atoms of definite finite size."[24] Einstein began with the idea that atoms do exist. Then he used his observations and knowledge and reasoned in steps to a conclusion. First, he had watched smoke from his pipe and the way tiny smoke particles dispersed. Second, he had the information about diffusion of sugar in water which he had researched for his second paper. Third, he drew on the 1828 study of Scottish botanist Robert Brown. Brown had dropped pollen grains into a liquid and observed that the pollen grains moved about in an agitated motion.

Then Einstein began to reason that tiny particles disperse. He theorized that if the dispersing particles are composed of smaller objects, as molecules or atoms, then the liquid they are dispersing in must also be composed of molecules or atoms. Then he thought that atoms in a liquid would move in the same agitated way that Brown found the pollen to move. But why? Einstein imagined the atoms in the liquid in two ways. If the liquid atoms bombarded the added atoms equally and regularly from all sides, they would not move. If the liquid atoms bombarded the added atoms in an irregular, or random, pattern, the added atoms would get tossed about, as the pollen grains had been. Einstein then reasoned that he could not predict how one atom would move, but over time the collective motion of the dispersing atoms would form a pattern, which could be calculated statistically. Just as it is impossible to predict if one coin toss will come up heads or tails, it is predictable that with many coin tosses, heads and tails will appear equally often.

Next he needed calculations, a formula that could be tested. Einstein used statistical averages and equations for determining rates of diffusion and compared the two. Banesh Hoffmann described Einstein's method:

Einstein found a novel method. He showed that if one waited, the random zigzags would give rise to migrations of various amounts. He pointed out that this migratory process was essentially a process of diffusion, such as he had studied in the case of sugar and water. By calculating it both ways—as random zigzag migration and as diffusion—and comparing the results, he found the formula he wanted.[25]

The result was a formula that experimenters could use to prove that atoms exist. This third paper became known as the paper on Brownian movement. Like his paper on light, this paper helped to form the basis for atomic and nuclear study, in particular Einstein's observation of random motion and his use of statistical averages. Even the skeptics, who had doubted that matter is composed of atoms, accepted the atom after the publication of this third paper.

The Fourth Paper

A month after the paper on Brownian movement, on June 30, 1905, Einstein's fourth paper called "On the Electrodynamics of Moving Bodies" reached *Annalen der Physik*. This was Einstein's first paper on relativity, the view of the universe Einstein is most famous for. Again he worked according to the same method: an idea, reasoning, and finding a formula. Einstein began with the idea that something was wrong with the Newtonian view of the clockwork universe and the idea of absolute time and space. If the universe was created by God and knowable only to God, he reasoned, then humans could never know anything for certain. If only God knows absolutely what time an event occurs and absolutely what the measurements are for distances and objects, then humans could never make accurate mea-

The Meaning of Space and Time

Einstein's special relativity theory has been widely misinterpreted. In an essay entitled "The Philosophical Significance of the Theory of Relativity," philosopher Hans Reichenbach explains philosophers' and Einstein's meaning of space and time. His essay appears in volume 1 of Albert Einstein: Philosopher-Scientist, *edited by Paul Arthur Schilpp:*

"The question of what is space and time has fascinated the authors of philosophical systems over and over again. Plato answered it by inventing a world of 'higher' reality, the world of ideas, which includes space and time among its ideal objects and reveals their relations to the mathematician who is able to perform the necessary act of vision. For Spinoza space was an attribute of God. Kant, on the other hand, denied the reality of space and time and regarded these two conceptual systems as forms of visualization, i.e., as constructions of the human mind, by means of which the human observer combines his perceptions so as to collect them into an orderly system.

The answer we can give to the question on the basis of Einstein's theory is very different from the answers of these philosophers. The theory of relativity shows that space and time are neither ideal objects nor forms of order necessary for the human mind. They constitute a relational system expressing certain features of physical objects and thus are descriptive of the physical world. Let us make this fact quite clear."

surements of any object nor know exactly when events happen. There must be a better way, he thought. Humans could know how fast something goes compared to a stationary object or compared to some other moving object. Humans can know the measurement of one object compared to some other object. That is, people can know things compared to, or relative to, other things. That idea gives the name to relativity theory.

Einstein first established two working definitions. Time, he said, is what we mea-

sure with clocks. Space is what we measure with measuring rods, or rulers. To find out where a moving object is and how fast it moves, he used two calculations that he could compare. For example, if a person in a train car walked in the same direction that the train moves, the train would seem to have one speed. If a person on the street watches the train go by, the train would seem to have a slightly slower speed. Both speeds could be measured at the same time. The result would be one speed compared to, or relative to, another. The problem was to find equations so that the formula would be useful to anyone who wanted to calculate a comparison between any two things.

Einstein used geometry. He used the usual three-dimensional measurements of height, length, and depth, but he added a fourth, a measurement for time. By adding time he could measure the speed of the train for the person inside the train car at the same time he could measure the speed of the train for the person on the street and have an accurate comparison. Still missing was a way to calculate the comparison. Einstein used the speed of light for the calculation because light travels at 186,000 miles per second regardless of the conditions. In other words, the speed of light is constant, which Einstein symbolized as c. (Einstein used the c as a constant for light just as Max Planck had used the h as a constant measure for heat.) By using one number, c, to apply to both measurements, he developed the formula for accurate measurements of objects in motion. The result is a measurement of space-time. Einstein explained that the basic idea of relativity "in its widest sense and in short and precise form is this: 'There is no absolute motion.'"[26]

This theory, which Einstein called the special theory of relativity because it was too incomplete to apply to every kind of measurement, baffled many scientists, but Einstein now had the answer to the question he had asked at sixteen. For years scientists and lay people were used to thinking that a train went at a definite speed of so many miles per hour. With this theory they had to think of the train going so many miles per hour from this perspective at this time. Further, after thinking for years about space *and* time, with this the-

ory they had to think in space-time, as one thing. If scientists were baffled, Einstein was clear about what would happen if a person could travel alongside a light beam. If she could, the light beam would appear to be standing still relative to her. But she could not travel with a light beam because *nothing* travels at the speed of light.

With Einstein's theory of relativity, scientists can make accurate measurements for long distances and for very high speeds. In reality, Newton's laws of motion worked accurately for measuring trains and for most calculations that study the earth and its surroundings. Newton's laws are inaccurate, however, for measurements of objects far out in space and for objects traveling at speeds, for example, of 90 percent of the speed of light.

The Fifth Paper

In September, three months after the special relativity paper, Einstein sent his fifth paper to *Annalen der Physik*. This paper, published in November, was three pages long. Einstein's fifth paper is sometimes considered a part of the relativity theory because Einstein used equations from the special relativity paper. Again Einstein was thinking about one thing relative to another, this time about mass relative to energy. Einstein began with the idea that mass and energy are equivalent, which means that two things have equal amounts even if they have different forms. (For example, a dollar bill is equivalent to four quarters; they have the same value, but have different forms.) Previously, scientists had thought energy and mass were separate and had developed separate laws for

Einstein's Confidence

Taking a broader view, science historian Gerald Holton, in The Advancement of Science, and Its Burdens, *asks what lessons Einstein's 1905 work taught. He finds answers in Einstein's vision and his character:*

"Einstein was not interested in easy victories, and dared to take great intellectual risks. . . . As he later remarked to his assistant Ernst Straus, 'What really interests me is whether God had any choice in the creation of the world.' This meant dispensing with everything that lacked the stamp of necessity. It meant suspecting and removing the barriers with which others had become comfortable—precisely the style of other figures that have played the same kind of cultural role: Copernicus giving up differences in the state of motion of the earth and the other planets, Galileo and Newton synthesizing terrestrial and celestial physics, Darwin stressing the continuity of *Homo sapiens* with other life forms, and Freud the psychological continuity of the child and the adult person and the conscious and unconscious mind.

A second lesson is that this young outsider took his ideas seriously. As noted, . . . this was tested quickly and in a striking way, for immediately upon the publication of Einstein's 1905 relativity paper there appeared in the *Annalen der Physik* an experimental test by the eminent experimentalist Walter Kaufmann, showing that his results appeared to contradict Einstein's theory. If Einstein had been a naive believer in the strategy of falsification, he might have accepted this disproof from a source of highest reputation, and gone on to other things: of course he did not.

The certainty with which this young man felt he was unpuzzling the design of the Creator becomes the more remarkable if one follows the story of Kaufmann's experiment further: It took ten years, to 1916, for it to be fully realized that, most surprisingly, Kaufmann's apparatus had been inadequate; apparently there was a leak in the vacuum system, which changed the effective fields available for deflecting the electron beam. By that time, the matter had been settled on other grounds."

each. With his new perspective, Einstein reasoned that if a body, a mass of something, gave off energy, then the size of the mass would diminish, according to the amount of energy given off. He thought that this idea would hold true for all forms of energy: heat, light, or electricity. To make a formula, he used E to symbolize energy and again he used c, the constant of light. His formula E/c^2 calculates the amount of mass that is lost relative to the amount of energy given off. According to this formula, a one-hundred-watt light bulb that burned (gave off energy) for one hundred years would lose less than a millionth of an ounce of mass, a very small amount.

In 1907 Einstein realized that the reverse is also true, that all mass is equivalent to energy. With this discovery, he was able to calculate the actual amount of conversion with the equation $E=mc^2$. If mass is equivalent to energy, does that mean that every stone, every lock of hair, every piece of glass is a body of trapped energy? Theoretically that may be true, but common objects do not convert to energy easily. Mass will convert to energy only at extremely high speeds or at extremely high temperatures. Twenty-five years after Einstein published this theory, scientists developed equipment that could propel atoms fast enough to test the theory, and the results confirmed Einstein's equation. Einstein thought that this theory was the most important result of special relativity.

This theory of the equivalence of mass and energy is the basis for splitting the atom and for making atomic bombs. The amount of mass that accrues when energy is converted is very small, but the amount of energy released from mass is enormous. When scientists discovered a way to split a uranium atom and start a chain reaction

Einstein's equation stating the equivalence of matter and energy floats eerily over glowing nuclear fuel rods. His theory led to the discovery of atomic energy.

of uranium atoms splitting, they had found a way to release a tremendous amount of energy and create a powerful explosion. With that knowledge scientists crafted a bomb. Einstein understood the potential destructive power of such a release of energy, but he thought many decades would pass before scientists would discover a way to release energy from mass. It happened in thirty-one years.

Privatdozent in Bern

After he published the five theories in 1905, Einstein received a promotion at the Patent Office from a third-class to a second-class technical expert, effective in April 1906. Working at the patent job, Einstein began thinking again about a university position, particularly because such a job would give him access to good libraries. First, however, he had to become a *privatdozent*, a requirement to be eligible for a professorship. A *privatdozent* is authorized to lecture at a university and charge small fees to those who attend in order to learn lecturing skills under the supervision of an experienced lecturer.

Since he lived in Bern, Einstein applied to be a *privatdozent* at the University of Bern and sent his paper on relativity as his credential. His application was rejected with an explanation that his paper was incomprehensible. He then applied to teach at a Zurich gymnasium, but Professor Kleiner, who had finally granted him a Ph.D., wanted Einstein to work at the University of Zurich. He encouraged Einstein to apply again to become a *privatdozent* at Bern University. Einstein reapplied and this time he was accepted. He began giving lectures on the science of heat, but prepared poorly and looked shabby. Only two students attended, his friend Besso, and another man from the Patent Office. When Professor Kleiner came to observe the class, he told Einstein that his lecture was poorly fitted to students' needs. Ein-

Einstein's Undaunted Spirit

Einstein possessed the will and the spirit to work and achieve results in spite of personal drawbacks. In an essay entitled "Einstein," excerpted from Einstein: The First Hundred Years, *C. P. Snow discusses Einstein's troubles in Prague which his spirit overcame:*

"In 1911 he [Einstein] went to a full chair at the German university in Prague. . . . There was, however, trouble in his home. No one knows how deeply it affected him. By the time he had moved to Prague, his marriage was going wrong. Altogether, the stay in Prague was an unhappy one. Einstein had to become a state official of the Hapsburg empire: in order to do this he had to declare his religion. He had lost all connections with Judaism: but anti-semitism was strong in Austria, and that was enough reason for Einstein to insist on registering himself—Israelite. His wife, Mileva, was sunk in melancholia: it didn't help that she was a Slav, in the midst of racial unrest.

Yet Einstein's laugh was still ringing out, his spirits were not yet damped. He was showing a new ability as an actor—with a touch of ham—on the lecture platform. There are pleasant stories of his playing the violin to a cultivated salon which discussed Kant . . . and enjoyed chamber music."

stein told him, "I don't demand to be appointed professor at Zurich,"[27] and recommended his friend Adler for the position. However, when Adler was offered the position, he declined and said:

> If it is possible to obtain a man like Einstein for our university, it would be absurd to appoint me. I must quite frankly say that my ability as a research physicist does not bear even the slightest comparison to Einstein's. Such an opportunity to obtain a man who could benefit us so much by raising the general level of the university should not be lost.[28]

Zurich chose Einstein as associate professor on May 7, 1909, when Einstein was thirty years old. He resigned from the Patent Office, effective October 1909, and moved to Zurich.

Assistant Professor in Zurich

Einstein began work as an assistant professor in the fall of 1909, but he soon had mixed feelings about his new job. He was at heart a humble man and hated the demands that social convention required of a professor. To avoid politicking for position and influence, he refused to mix socially or at meetings with other professors, though he enjoyed discussing scientific problems with his colleagues. Biographer Anton Reiser explained that Einstein was a good private tutor, but not a good lecturer. He said:

> A lecturing professor, however, is hardly ever able to influence his students directly and almost never meets them personally. He stands, an expert at his lecturer's table, represents discipline, and is supposed to present his doctrine and his researches to the students. Activities of this nature—the end and aim of most professors—at first held forth very little promise for young Albert. He showed a definite timidity, which even today he has not overcome, towards speaking in public. He always called his lectures "performances on the trapeze." His nature, which above all enjoyed being alone, or with his work in the silence of his own room, found his professorial activities hardly pleasant.[29]

While Einstein was poor at grinding out regular lectures, he always had time to help students. He told them, "I shall always be able to receive you. If you have a problem, come to me with it. You will never disturb me, since I can interrupt my work at a moment and resume it immediately."[30]

Being a university professor made few changes in his personal life. During the first year in Zurich, his second son Eduard was born, and Einstein continued to wheel his children through the streets of the city. He still had few personal needs and little desire for power and advantages, but he needed to support his wife and two boys. With the same income that he had had in the Patent Office, he now had more expenses. He said, "In my relativity theory I set up a clock at every point in space, but in reality I find it difficult to provide even one clock in my room."[31]

Even though he was now a man of position, he treated everyone alike: leading officials, the grocer, and the scrubwoman in the laboratory. This behavior made high-ranking professors uncomfortable.

In 1911 Einstein (standing second from right) was asked to participate in the prestigious Solvay Congress in Brussels, Belgium. The invitation to the conference, which included other highly respected scientists such as Marie Curie (seated second from right) signalled the scientific community's growing respect for Einstein.

Full Professor in Prague

His life in Zurich, however, lasted only a short period. Max Planck, the German physicist responsible for the publication of *Annalen der Physik* in 1905, was on the committee to search for new professors for the German University in Prague, in what is today The Czech Republic, and he wanted Einstein as a full professor because he would bring prestige to the school. Max Planck said, "If Einstein's theory should prove to be correct, as I expect it will, he will be considered the Copernicus of the twentieth century."[32] In 1911 Einstein accepted a position as full professor at the German University in Prague. Einstein was at first delighted to have the opportunity to use an outstanding library, but he soon found that his new job and all the duties that went with full professorship left him little peace for his own work, and he longed for the quiet hours at the Patent Office. He felt more and more that a life away from people, a contemplative existence such as artists have, was the kind of life he preferred, but he took the trappings of academic life in good humor. For example, professors had uniforms for special occasions—a three-cornered hat with feathers, a coat and trousers decorated with wide gold bands, a heavy black overcoat, and a sword. Einstein's son Hans Albert wanted his dad to wear the uniform as he walked through the streets. Einstein complied, saying, "I don't mind; at most, people will think I'm a Brazilian admiral." [33]

Full Professor at Polytechnic

Other events indicated that Einstein's respect among scientists was growing. In the fall of 1911, Einstein was one of twenty-one select scientists invited to speak at the Solvay Congress in Brussels, Belgium. Ernest Solvay, a wealthy industrialist, sponsored the conference. In 1912 Einstein was offered professorships at four universities, in Utrect, Germany; Leiden, Netherlands; Vienna, Austria; and the Zurich Polytechnic. Since he liked Zurich, he chose his former university, where he had once failed the entrance exams and had been rejected for a teaching position. While working at university jobs, he also worked on several theories, the most important being the general relativity theory. He knew that his special relativity theory was a partial theory, and he wanted a more inclusive one, but it required a different kind of calculus. When he moved to Zurich, he sought help from his friend Marcel Grossman, who was a mathematics professor at the Polytechnic. Grossman's

help speeded up the work on the new theory, and the men published two papers on their cooperative work.

Invitation to Berlin

Although Einstein had been offered a ten-year position at Zurich Polytechnic starting in October 1912, Max Planck again visited him with an offer for the best position in Europe for a theoretical physicist. The job had three parts: the directorship of the Institute of Physics at the Kaiser Wilhelm Institute, a chair (a special position) at the Prussian Academy, and a professorship at the University of Berlin. Einstein

The title page from the first published edition of Einstein and Grossman's paper on general relativity.

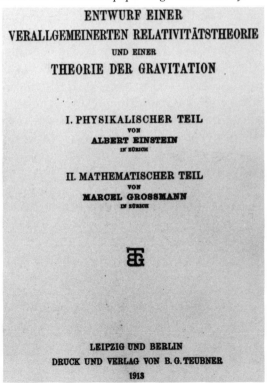

ENTWURF EINER
VERALLGEMEINERTEN RELATIVITÄTSTHEORIE
UND EINER
THEORIE DER GRAVITATION

I. PHYSIKALISCHER TEIL
VON
ALBERT EINSTEIN
IN ZÜRICH

II. MATHEMATISCHER TEIL
VON
MARCEL GROSSMANN
IN ZÜRICH

LEIPZIG UND BERLIN
DRUCK UND VERLAG VON B. G. TEUBNER
1913

Einstein's family (left to right), Eduard, Mileva, and Hans, unwillingly moved from their home in Zurich, Switzerland, to Berlin, Germany, in 1914.

was not interested in the prestige that came with the honorary titles, but several aspects of the job did appeal to him. First, the salary would allow him to live comfortably. Second, he would work with the leading scientists in Europe. And, third and best of all, he could teach only when he wanted to, leaving him time to work on the general relativity theory, a difficult task that required time for concentration and work on equations. There were two arguments against taking the job. First, Einstein was hesitant to go back to Ger-

many to work with the people who had made him uneasy as a child. Secondly, his wife Mileva liked Zurich and wanted to stay there; his relationship with her, however, had deteriorated into an unhappy situation. In the end, Einstein decided to accept the position he had been offered. In April 1914, he and his family left Switzerland for Berlin. Einstein had now reached the top of his profession, had become known to scientists around the world, and had a job that gave him the conditions to finish another revolutionary theory.

4 Berlin, General Relativity, and Fame: 1914-1920

The position Einstein began in April 1914, made him a director, a chair, and a professor all within the same job. The institute that he was to direct had been founded in 1911, on the occasion of the University of Berlin's one-hundredth anniversary. Founded by economic leaders and supported by the state, the institute was set up as part of the Kaiser Wilhelm Society for the Advancement of Science. The Berlin Academy, the oldest scientific institution in Germany, had had some of the greatest German scholars as its members. In his position as a chair, Einstein was expected to do research. He expected the job of directing to take little time. Biographer Anton Reiser described the academy's purpose:

> The Academy is concerned not with teaching but with investigation. Its regular members are for the most part professors of the University of Berlin or of other universities . . . [hired] to devote their entire time to scientific work. It was this type of professorship that Albert Einstein accepted in 1914. It is an office for the scientific investigator, while his teaching activity at the university is more a right than a duty. . . . The Academy is, nevertheless, the highest authority in scholarly circles. It publishes the work of its members, supports important research, arranges for the publication of important works, both old and new, and offers prizes. In fact, next to the university, which is concerned with instruction, it is the most important center of learning.[34]

Einstein, at forty, in his study in Berlin. Though he held the most prestigious position available to a theoretical physicist, Einstein most valued the time for research that the position gave him.

Einstein's Distaste for Academic Politics

Einstein worried that he might not "lay an egg" in his new job in Berlin. In Einstein: His Life and Times, *biographer Phillip Frank describes the daily topics of conversation that were usual among professors the world over. Einstein had no interest in such topics:*

"Einstein's solitary position in academic circles was due also to the fact that he did not like to take part in the problems of professional daily life; he was unable to take them seriously. The daily life of a scholar is often a matter of discussing and becoming excited about the frequency with which his papers are published, which colleagues have or have not published anything, which colleague has frequently or infrequently cited which other colleague, or who intentionally or unintentionally has failed to cite somebody else. There are discussions of the merits of individual professors, the honors that they have or have not received from their own or other universities, and the academies to which they have been elected. Then again the conversation may turn to the number of students for whom the professors have been able to obtain positions, the students and teachers whom they have been able to prevent from obtaining positions, whether they have any influence with superior officials, and whether they are able to obtain money for their department from these authorities.

Taken as a whole, all these problems add up to a tremendous total of interests and intellectual effort, in which Einstein hardly participated. It would be very unjust to maintain that all these conversations are valueless for scientific activity. On the contrary, they have their justification in social life. Nevertheless, too much attention to these details may prevent one from dealing with the actual problems of science."

In spite of the financial security the job offered, he had some apprehension about what was expected of him. At a farewell dinner in Zurich, he described himself as a prize hen, gambled on by the gentlemen of Berlin. He worried that he did not know if he would lay another golden egg. At the time he was having trouble with the mathematics in his general theory and felt unsure that he could solve the problems and complete the theory. He expressed his uncertainty again when he gave his inaugural address to the academy. He said:

Separation from Mileva

Over the next few months, there were several changes in Einstein's life. In the summer of 1914, only a few months after the Einsteins had moved to Berlin, Mileva returned to Zurich to visit her family, taking the two boys with her. Then in August of that year, World War I broke out, and it seemed unsafe for Mileva to return. Einstein did not care. Their relationship had become stormy, and Einstein needed peace in order to think and work. He spent the holidays that year with fellow scientists in Berlin. During the war years Einstein stayed with his father's cousin Rudolph Einstein, who had married the sister of his mother. He became reacquainted with their daughter Elsa, who had visited the Einsteins in Munich and who was now a widow with two teenage daughters, Ilse and Margot.

Einstein's cousin Elsa, who later became his second wife.

First of all I have to thank you most heartily for conferring on me the greatest boon that could be conferred on a man like myself. By electing me to your Academy you have freed me from the distractions and cares of a professional life and so made it possible for me to devote myself entirely to scientific studies. I hope that you will continue to believe in my gratitude and industry even when my efforts appear to yield only poor results.[35]

Thus, he began working as a director, doing his own research, and giving others advice on their research.

Breakthrough Does Not Come Easily

Einstein tried to keep the war from interfering with his life and work, naively believing that science had nothing to do with politics. He was shocked, however, to see his German colleagues enthusiastically help with the war efforts, and get involved in such tasks as developing chemical weapons. For him, the war had the opposite effect. He became even more committed to internationalism (world government), and pacifism (the opposition to war and violence as a means to settle disputes), but he only occasionally spoke out. His work was particularly difficult at the time, and because he knew his job was financed by men with whom he disagreed politically, he immersed himself in the work to minimize conflict. He had been working on the general relativity theory for eight years. While Einstein still worked in Zurich, his friend Marcel Grossman had helped him with the mathematics. But now Einstein struggled alone, faced with a set of ten equations that he and Grossman had developed. Einstein hoped to find a way to bring all ten equations together. After trying for two years to reach a solution, he found the summer of 1915 particularly agonizing. Finally, he took a fresh approach and assigned all the equations an equal value. When he realized that the new approach was correct, progress was quick. Everything fell into place with beautiful simplicity. He had found a new theory of gravity based on the ten equations, the general theory of relativity that he had sought for so long. He completed the theory in November 1915. He wrote to a friend, "In all my life I have never before labored so hard. Compared with this problem, the original theory of relativity is child's play."[36]

The general theory of relativity is Einstein's greatest achievement, nearly fulfilling a goal set years ago in Munich. As a youth, his fascination with the compass, science books, and what a light beam was made of had fueled his curiosity about the workings of the universe. So far, he had achieved special relativity, a partial explanation of these workings, and general relativity, a more unified picture of the universe. Though the general relativity theory was a great accomplishment, Einstein, however, knew that it was not the complete theory that he hoped to find in the future.

Ideas and Assumptions for General Relativity

Einstein developed the general relativity theory by the same method he had used for his previous theories: he began with an

These four equations express Einstein's theory of gravity, the heart of his general theory of relativity. The theory presents a completely new way of looking at the universe, as radically new as Copernicus's had been in the sixteenth century.

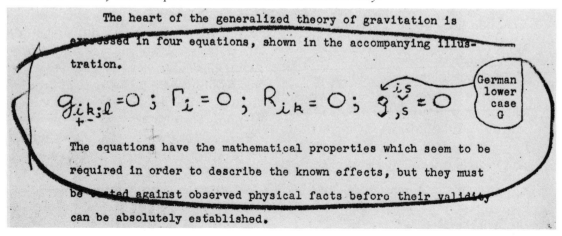

$$\mathcal{E}\mathcal{L} = mc^2 + \frac{m}{2}q^2 + \cdots \qquad (28')$$

A page from Einstein's manuscript in which he worked out his theory of relativity.

idea, reasoned according to ideas and principles, developed equations, and provided methods for testing the theory. Einstein began with the idea that Newton's law of gravity was wrong, that gravity was not a force pulling objects toward the center of a body. He developed the theory out of two ideas and based it on two assumptions. His first idea was that space is not merely an empty background for events, but possesses a structure of its own. His second idea was that gravity is not a pulling force, but it is a function of matter itself; that is, gravity is closely related to and dependent on matter. From these ideas he guided his work on the basis of two assumptions. First, he assumed that matter and energy are equivalent, as he stated in his fifth paper published in 1905. Second, he assumed the principle of covariance, the principle that the laws of physics have the same form regardless of the system of coordinates in which they are expressed. In other words, the laws of physics do not change even when a physicist uses the law with different sets of specific numbers. Banesh Hoffmann expresses his appreciation for Einstein's work in these words: "By what magical clairvoyance did Einstein choose just these two principles to be his guide long before he knew where they would lead him? That they should have led him to unique equations of so complex yet simple a sort is itself astounding."[37]

The general theory of relativity contains difficult mathematical equations and new concepts about the universe. According to Stephen Hawking, Einstein suggests that

gravity is not a force like other forces, but is a consequence of the fact that space-time is not flat, as had been previously assumed: it is curved, or "warped," by the distribution of mass and energy in it. Bodies like the earth are not made to move on curved orbits by a force called gravity; instead, they follow the nearest thing to a straight path in curved space, which is called a geodesic. A geodesic is the shortest (or longest) path between two nearby points.[38]

Accepting Einstein's Complex View

In his final lecture entitled "Summary and Outlook," published in Albert Einstein and the Cosmic World Order, *Cornelius Lanczos explains the significance of the evolution from Newton's to Einstein's order of the world:*

"If before [in special relativity], time was absorbed by space, now matter became absorbed by space, giving us a new physical world picture in which matter appeared as a certain curvature property of the space-time world. . . . We can regret the fact that so many of our cherished ideas concerning space, time and matter had to be thrown overboard. How simple was the picture of the physical world before Einstein's relativity and quantum theory appeared on the scene. We could go a long way with the simple concepts of force, work, energy, and a few similar ideas. Today the picture of the physical world is infinitely more complex. Where Newton succeeded with one single quantity, Einstein introduced *ten* quantities and the relations between these quantities is by far more complex than the simple equation found by Newton. Should we not deplore then the passing of the naive phase of physics, comparable to the golden age of mankind, spent in a paradisiac innocence of fairy tales? Today, from the perspective of history, the evolution from Newton to Einstein appears to us in a different light. We admit the loss of simplicity, but we are willing to pay the price for the sake of the tremendous advance in *unity.*"

In other words, says Timothy Ferris, with the theory of relativity, Einstein created a "geometry of space itself: Matter curves space. . . . The planets skid along the inner walls of a depression in space created by the fat, massive sun; clusters of galaxies rest in spatial hollows like nuggets in a prospector's bowl."[39] To develop equations for this theory, Einstein was unable to use Euclidean geometry, which has laws for straight lines, flat surfaces, and right angles. He needed a geometry for curved spaces and geodesic angles. He used the mathematical laws of Reimann's geometry, the mathematics that Marcel Grossman had helped him with. For the mathematician "curvature" has to do with the geometry of space, not its shape, as nonmathematicians are likely to think. This theory presented a radically new way of thinking about the universe, as well as complex and difficult mathematical equations.

Predictions in General Relativity

For Einstein, a scientific theory was more than an intuitive truth, logically reasoned ideas, and equations. It also had to be proved with experiments that showed the theory to be true. The general theory of relativity made four predictions that could be tested and verified. First, it predicted a measure of planet Mercury's orbit. Because Mercury is the planet nearest the sun, its orbit is slightly different from the orbits of the other planets, and Newton's equations were wrong for Mercury. Einstein applied his theory to Mercury's orbit and found that it was accurate.

Second, the theory predicted the curvature of space-time. This prediction could be verified by measuring the light from a distant star as it passed near the sun. Since the light from a distant star cannot be seen when the sun shines, measurement of the way light bends around the sun's mass could only be measured during a total eclipse, which occurred in 1919.

Third, the theory predicted a red shift. The scale used to show frequencies of light has a range from blue on one end, showing that objects are moving toward the observer, to red on the other end, showing that objects are moving away from the observer. Einstein's theory predicted that objects far out in the universe would have frequencies shifting toward red; that is, moving farther out. (American astronomer Edwin Hubble, who worked at Mount Wilson Observatory in California, verified Einstein's prediction of a red shift in 1929.)

Fourth, the theory predicted the existence of gravitational waves, ripples in the curvature of space emitted because heavy objects move. According to the theory, these waves travel at the speed of light. Still unverified in 1993, gravitational waves are the hardest of Einstein's predictions to verify because elaborate technology is necessary to detect the waves.

Late in 1915 Einstein announced to the Prussian Academy of Sciences that his theory showed accurately the orbit of Mercury. Newton's equations had shown a forty to fifty seconds of arc per century that scientists could not explain. Einstein told the academy that his new theory provided an additional advance for Mercury of approximately forty-three seconds of arc per century. In Einstein's calculations of the motion of the perihelion (the point of its orbit nearest the sun) of Mercury, there was no room for fudging and no need for adjustment. The precise outcome of this measurement signified the success of the theory. Einstein's announcement appeared in the academy's published *Proceedings*. In January Einstein wrote to his friend Paul Ehrenfest in Holland expressing his joy that his equations were accurate for the perihelion of Mercury.

The theory, along with its predictions, was published in the spring of 1916 in the *Annalen der Physik* with the title "Foundation of the General Theory of Relativity." German physicist Max Born described his initial reaction to the theory this way:

> The theory appeared to me then, and it still does, the greatest feat of human thinking about nature, the most amazing combination of philosophical penetration, physical intuition, and mathematical skill. But its connections with experience were slender. It appealed to me like a great work of art, to be enjoyed and admired from a distance.[40]

Einstein sent a copy of the journal containing his theory to William de Sitter, professor of astronomy at the University of Leiden in the Netherlands. De Sitter, a foreign correspondent of the Royal Astronomical Society in London, passed on his copy to Arthur Eddington, the society's secretary. In 1916, Eddington was a professor of astronomy at Cambridge University in England and director of the university observatory. Eddington asked de Sitter to write three long articles explaining the theory for the Royal Astronomical Society's monthly newsletter. These articles introduced Einstein's theory to the non-German-speaking world. Eddington made plans to test the theory at the time of the next appropriate eclipse, which would oc-

Cambridge professor of astronomy, Arthur Eddington, then secretary of the Royal Astronomical Society in London, introduced Einstein's general relativity theory to the English-speaking world in 1916.

cur in 1919. But the war caused difficulties for scientists and they had to be politically cautious; England, the homeland of Eddington, was on the opposite side of Germany, the homeland of Einstein.

Publications After General Relativity

In 1916 and 1917 after the general theory had been published, Einstein went on working and wrote two more papers and a book. In one paper, Einstein added a modification to the general theory, but it was wrong and he withdrew it later. In the other paper he showed how to arrive at Max Planck's heat-quantum law from a different starting point. In 1917 this revision of Planck's theory seemed of interest only to theoretical physicists, but the theory became useful forty years later in developing the laser of modern technology. In 1916 a publisher had asked Einstein to write an explanation of the general relativity theory that readers not trained in physics could understand. Since paper was scarce during the war, he compressed the theory into a book of seventy pages and wrote a simpler version of the mathematics. The first edition appeared in 1917, sold out, and went through a second printing. In 1918, when the publisher asked for a third printing of three thousand copies, Germany was hard-pressed and losing the war, but managed to make the paper available for Einstein's book.

The years 1917 to 1920 brought several changes in Einstein's personal life. He had begun negotiating a divorce from Mileva, making several trips to Zurich to discuss a settlement that would provide for

Mileva and the boys. Einstein found these trips exhausting because there were conflicts with Mileva and because he worried about his sons and felt sad to leave them. In 1917 he became ill. He had been working alone and intensely for over three years, eating poorly and sleeping at irregular hours. Doctors diagnosed his illness as stomach problems coupled with exhaustion. During his recovery his cousin Elsa cared for him and organized the details of his life. Einstein's friend Michele Besso took over the negotiations with Mileva, which eventually included an agreement that money from the anticipated Nobel Prize would go to her. Einstein gradually recovered from his illness. On February 14, 1919, his divorce was settled, and on June 2, 1919, he married Elsa. As Einstein's wife, Elsa respected her husband's scientific work and took on the role of organizing a life that gave Einstein undisturbed time, a healthy daily routine, and periodic recreation. Late in 1919, Einstein's mother Pauline was diagnosed with terminal cancer and came to Berlin to live with her son and Elsa. Einstein's mother died in February 1920, leaving Einstein feeling as desolate as he had when his father died many years earlier. In the meantime the war had ended in November 1918, with Germany's defeat.

Albert and Elsa Einstein were married in 1919. Elsa provided the care and organization the absent-minded Albert needed to remain healthy and free to work.

Verification of General Relativity

During the same time period British astronomers had gone forward with plans to test Einstein's prediction that a light beam from a distant star would bend around the sun's mass. A full eclipse occurred at two places in the Southern Hemisphere on May 29, 1919, one at Sobral in northern Brazil and another on the Principe Island in the Gulf of Guinea off the coast of Africa. Teams, including Arthur Eddington and British astronomer Royal Frank Dyson, went to both places in the event that clouds covered the sun on that day in one of the places. Both teams took photos of the eclipse through a telescope, and when the teams had evaluated both sets,

Elsa's Help and Support

In Albert Einstein: A Biographical Portrait, *Anton Reiser (a pseudonym for Elsa Einstein's son-in-law, Rudolf Kayser) describes the role Elsa played in Einstein's life and the peace and order she brought to him:*

"Frau Einstein finds it her duty to further with all her energy the life most suited to the character and tasks of her husband. It is a scholar's life, yet susceptible to all contemporary problems and to all human affairs. Both husband and wife are one in their constant readiness to help people with word and deed. Frau Einstein holds her husband's work to be a realm of great dignity and deep seriousness. She recognizes the need for keeping all disturbing elements away from him, especially when he is working on new problems which require his entire energy. She knows also that the strain of intellectual activity requires a counterpoise of good-fellowship in which the leading personalities of all countries meet. Here also well-known musicians often gather and play classical music with the head of the household."

Scientists photographed a 1919 eclipse of the sun to prove Einstein's prediction that distant starlight would bend around the sun's mass. The photos proved the theory correct.

they found that the photos confirmed Einstein's prediction. Eddington sent the news to Einstein's friend Hendrik Lorentz in the neutral country Holland, and Lorentz sent the news on to Einstein. On September 27, 1919, Einstein was meeting with a student in his office when the telegram from Lorentz arrived. Einstein handed her the telegram. She read it and exclaimed about the happy result, to which Einstein responded that he knew that the theory was correct. When the student asked Einstein what he would have thought had the results not confirmed the theory, Einstein told her, "Then I would have to be sorry for dear God. The theory is correct."[41]

Lorentz announced the results to a handful of professors in October, and the public announcement came on November

6, 1919, at a joint meeting of the Royal Society and the Royal Astronomical Society in London. Anticipating the announcement, mathematician and philosopher Alfred Whitehead said the atmosphere in the hall was tense, like that of a Greek drama. A world view was about to be overturned. And then Royal Society president J.J. Thomson rose to address the meeting. He spoke of Einstein's theory as "one of the greatest achievements in the history of human thought. . . . It is not the discovery of an outlying island but of a whole continent of new scientific ideas," he said. "It is the greatest discovery in connection with gravitation since Newton enunciated his principles."[42] Following Thomson's announcement, Dyson reported on the test and concluded that light deflected around the sun's gravitational field as predicted by Einstein's theory. On November 7, 1919, the headline in the *London Times* read: "Revolution in Science. Newtonian Ideas Overthrown."

Immediate Fame

On November 7, 1919, Einstein immediately became famous. All day reporters streamed in to visit him. Although he sincerely disliked the bother, he made a bargain with reporters. They had to contribute to a benefit fund for starving Viennese children, and then he allowed photos and gave statements. Einstein told Max Born that the publicity was so bad that he could hardly breathe, let alone do any work. In the following days sackloads of letters poured in, invitations arrived from foreign countries to visit and to lecture, and countless causes asked for Einstein's

support and for money. Sales of his little seventy-page book skyrocketed, and translations appeared in many languages. Book salesmen needed a brief summary to explain the theory since some folks seemed to think relativity was about relations between the sexes. The *London Times* supplement published three, full-page articles on the theory. In London the House of Commons started an Einstein Society. Arthur Eddington lectured on the theory in Cambridge and hundreds had to be turned away, not even able to get near the room. In Paris *Scientific American* sponsored an essay contest on the theory. Palladium music hall in London offered to pay any price to have Einstein play his violin there. A cigar

Einstein poses with the colleagues who publicized his general theory of relativity (left to right from top) Einstein, William de Sitter, Paul Ehrenfest, Arthur Eddington, and Hendrik Lorentz.

In 1919, Einstein became world famous and, consequently, the subject of writers, artists, and cartoonists worldwide.

layers of scientists, the academic community at large, professionals, workers, and the common people on the street, Einstein aroused attention in all, and awe and near hysteria in some. In a letter dated February 20, 1920, Einstein wrote to a friend:

> Saying "no" has never been a strong point with me, but in my present distress I am at last gradually learning the art. Since the flood of newspaper articles, I have been so swamped with questions, invitations, challenges, that I dream that I am burning in Hell and that the postman is the Devil eternally roaring at me, throwing new bundles of letters at my head because I have not yet answered the old ones.[43]

Leopold Infeld, who worked with Einstein many years later, said that he was a school teacher in a small Polish town when Einstein became famous, and he did what multitudes of science teachers did all over the world—he gave a lecture on the theory of relativity. On a cold winter night a large crowd lined up, so large that it could not fit into the biggest hall in the town. Infeld said that Einstein's photograph appeared in newspaper after newspaper. "To my astonishment I saw a face more of an artist and a prophet than that of a scientist."[44] Einstein was well on his way to becoming a legend.

manufacturer marketed an Einstein cigar. Parents named their children after him. Cartoonists drew him in caricature.

Einstein's fame spread around the world with great speed. Down through the

Chapter

5 Recognition, Misconceptions, and Causes: 1920-1933

Einstein lived in Berlin for nearly nineteen years. During his first six years in that city, his divorce and remarriage, his general relativity theory and its verification all

Two stars of modern physics, Max Planck and Albert Einstein, share a moment during one of the numerous award ceremonies given for Einstein.

marked dramatic changes, but his life was focused on a few events. The 1919 verification, however, set the world astir. In the years following 1920, attention rained on Einstein like a shower of confetti, most of it to honor him. His life was filled with innumerable details of honors, speeches, travels, awards, letters, requests, causes, and a few attacks. Unworldly in spite of world fame, Einstein was often amused and sometimes baffled by all the attention afforded him, but he tried his best to please, accommodate, and fulfill his responsibilities.

Einstein's Honors

Einstein's honors came in many forms. By 1920 his book *Relativity: The Special and the General Theory* had gone through fourteen German editions, totaling 65,000 copies. The English translation went through seven editions in nineteen months. By 1921 a bibliography on relativity included 650 papers, articles, and books. In addition to the volumes written about his theory, words of praise came from leading scientists. For example, a German physicist said there were two kinds of physicists in Berlin: there was Einstein and there were all the others. When Einstein appeared at King's College, London, Lord Haldane said, "You see here before you . . . the Newton of the twentieth century, a man who has called forth a greater revolution of thought than even Copernicus, Galileo, or Newton himself."[45] Furthermore, when Einstein went to universities to speak, many conferred honorary degrees on him. By 1921 he had lost count of the number of doctoral degrees he had received, an ironic situation for a man who had trouble getting his first one. In addition to degrees, Einstein received medals

Einstein lecturing at Leiden University in the Netherlands. He was flooded with requests to speak all over the world.

of honor: for example, the English Royal Society's Copley Medal, the Royal Astronomical Society's Gold Medal, and the first German Max Planck Medal, all of them the most prestigious medals offered.

Einstein Is Famous

During the first few years following verification of general relativity, Einstein had more invitations to speak than he could accept. At the University of Leiden, Netherlands, he lectured to fourteen hundred students. To gain privacy from reporters during his visit to Prague to lecture at the German University, the Einsteins stayed with Professor Frank and his wife in Einstein's old office. In Vienna, Austria, he lectured to three thousand people who came in such a state of excitement, it seemed as if they cared not whether they understood the lecture so long as they could be near the man of miracles. Einstein thought all the fame was nonsense and refused to change his habits or style of dress because of it. Einstein's Viennese hostess, a proper woman, bought Einstein slippers and sent his pants to be pressed, but Einstein wore his wrinkled ones and never wore the slippers. When he went to lecture in France, Germany's war enemy, Einstein had to travel in secret. He also lectured in England and Sweden.

Attacks and Danger

While the world and leading scientists were praising Einstein, German political and scientific extremists attacked him vi-

Manifesto for Peace and World Unity

"Technology has shrunk the world. Indeed, today the nations of the great European peninsula seem to jostle one another much as once did the city-states that were crowded into those smaller peninsulas jutting out into the Mediterranean. Travel is so widespread, international supply and demand are so interwoven, that Europe—one could almost say the whole world—is even now a single unit.

Surely, it is the duty of Europeans of education and goodwill at least to try to prevent Europe from succumbing, because of lack of international organization, to the fate that once engulfed ancient Greece! Or will Europe also suffer slow exhaustion and death by fratricidal war?

The struggle raging today can scarcely yield a 'victor'; all nations that participate in it will, in all likelihood, pay an exceedingly high price. Hence it appears not only wise but imperative for men of education in all countries to exert their influence for the kind of peace treaty that will not carry the seeds of future wars, whatever the outcome of the present conflict may be. The unstable and fluid situation in Europe, created by the war, must be utilized to weld the continent into an organic whole. Technically and intellectually, conditions are ripe for such a development.

This is not the place to discuss how this new order in Europe may be brought about. Our sole purpose is to affirm our profound conviction that the time has come when Europe must unite to guard its soil, its people, and its culture. We are stating publicly our faith in European unity, a faith which we believe is shared by many; we hope that this public affirmation of our faith may contribute to the growth of a powerful movement toward such unity."

ciously. Hurt by war losses and punishments imposed by war enemies, many Germans were angry and looked for someone to blame. Some resented Einstein for refusing to work for the war and for his opinions on pacifism and internationalism. Outspoken extremists and a few scientists created "The Study Group of Natural Philosophers," a group that paid fees to anyone willing to publicly criticize Einstein's theory or his character. The group displayed large posters advertising their meetings. Out of curiosity, Einstein attended one and laughed at the outrageous comments made about him and his theory. A reputable scientist from Heidelberg, Germany, Philip Lenard, led another attack on Einstein. He attacked Einstein's physics and claimed that relativity was a Jewish plot to change and corrupt the world. In June 1922, right-wing extremists killed government minister Walther Rathenau, a Jewish intellectual and friend of Einstein's. On the day of Rathenau's funeral, an official day of mourning, all universities closed, but Lenard held lectures in defiance. Two days later, attackers seriously wounded another prominent Jew, Maximilian Harden. Ger-

(Top) Einstein the professor, the year he won the Nobel Prize. (Left) Elsa and Albert, in 1921, now well off.

man Rudolph Leibus, who had earlier offered a reward for the murder of Einstein, was finally charged and convicted, but his punishment was a fine that amounted to less than twenty dollars! Following Rathenau's assassination, rumors spread that Einstein was also on the list of intended victims. Because of the growing anti-Semitism Einstein considered leaving Berlin in the early 1920s and settling in Leiden, Netherlands, but he decided to stay to fight against nationalism and to support Jews. He predicted that he would be able to stay in Germany no longer than another ten years.

Two Long Trips

On their first trip abroad, the Einsteins traveled to America to help raise money for Zionism, a movement to establish a homeland for Jews, but Americans had planned more than a fundraiser. On April 2, 1921, the Einsteins arrived in America by boat to find hoards of reporters coming aboard for a press conference. Besides his photo, reporters wanted Einstein to sum up relativity in a few sentences and explain why the theory was so popular. He told them that relativity would not change the life of the man on the street. He said:

> If you will not take the answer too seriously and consider it only as a kind of joke, then I can explain it as follows. It was formerly believed that if all material things disappeared out of the universe, time and space would be left. According to the relativity theory, however, time and space disappear together with the things.[46]

Along with other guests, the Einsteins pose on the White House lawn next to President Warren G. Harding. Einstein had been invited to speak to the National Academy of Sciences in Washington, D.C.

He answered reporters' questions and hoped he had stood up well to the scrutiny. However, the press conference was only the beginning. He had dinners and tours with New York's mayor, New York's future governor, and the city council president. One fund-raising meeting collected $26,000, with pledges for another $100,000. He lectured on relativity at Columbia University and New York University. He went to Washington, D.C., as a guest of President Harding and spoke to the National Academy of Sciences. He lectured at Princeton University, where he received an honorary degree, and traveled to Chicago, Cleveland, and Boston. Most of the time Einstein found it an amusing nuisance that people who had little real interest in science and less understanding of it were creating such a hubbub. In spite of all the attention, he remained humble and shy. He told a Boston audience that "when a man after years of searching chances upon a thought which discloses something of the beauty of this mysterious universe he should not therefore be personally celebrated. He is already suffi-ciently paid by his experience in seeking and finding."[47] From Boston the Einsteins returned to Berlin after a stop in England, where Einstein lectured and tried to reconcile war animosities between Germany and England.

Celebrity in Japan

In the fall of 1922, the Einsteins' trip to Japan kept them equally busy with lectures, appearances, and honors. They stopped in Colombo, the capital of Ceylon (now

---

Einstein as Peacemaker

In Albert Einstein: Creator and Rebel, *Banesh Hoffmann describes how the force of Einstein's personality affected British enmity toward Germany:*

"On his way back from America he stopped briefly in England, where he had been invited to lecture at the University of Manchester and at King's College of London University. Feelings in England against Germany still ran high, and no one could tell beforehand what might happen at Einstein's lecture. Einstein spoke in German, the still-hated enemy tongue—and his lectures were received enthusiastically. By the sheer force of his personality, by his naturalness, his simplicity, his humor, his mastery of his subject, and the indefinable aura of greatness that no diffidence of his could hide, he captivated his audiences. All during his stay he was treated as a veritable hero of the mind. Manchester University bestowed on him an honorary doctorate. In London the Einsteins stayed as honored guests in the home of the statesman and philosopher Viscount Haldane. There and elsewhere Einstein met many of Britain's notables. And all in all, as Haldane and Einstein both had hoped, the visit greatly furthered the cause of international reconciliation."

The Einsteins during their world travels in 1921. Albert lectured in America, Japan, China, France, and Spain.

called Sri Lanka, an island in the Indian Ocean), and in Shanghai, China. In Japan Einstein lectured first at Tokyo University to a large audience of scholars, teachers, and students. He began speaking at 1:30 P.M. and spoke for three hours. After an hour's break, he spoke for another three hours to attentive listeners. For his second appearance, Einstein reduced his lecture by half, and the crowd was offended for getting less than the first audience. The Japanese, who paid all expenses for this trip, introduced the Einsteins to the emperor and empress, showed them gardens, took them to festivals, and held receptions in their honor, as well as taking Einstein to several cities for additional lectures. On the return trip the Einsteins stopped in Palestine, where Einstein gave the inaugural address at the newly founded Hebrew University. They stopped in Marseilles,

France, and in Barcelona and Madrid, Spain. At every stop he gave lectures on relativity. On the train from Madrid to Berlin, Einstein was tired of being a celebrity; he left Elsa in the first-class quarters and went to ride third class, where he tried to blend in with the crowd unnoticed.

The Nobel Prize

While Einstein was in Japan, he learned that the Swedish Academy of Science had awarded him the Nobel Prize in physics. Aware of the controversy that the relativity theory was causing in Germany, the academy carefully followed the rules set down for prizes; that is, the prize was for a discovery from which humanity had derived great use. Since humanity had yet to

Silent film star Charlie Chaplin, flanked by Albert and Elsa Einstein, his personal guests, arrives at a Hollywood movie theater to watch the premier of his latest movie in 1931.

derive great use from relativity, the academy awarded Einstein the prize for his photoelectric theory, his particle theory on light, which had use, but was not controversial. Another issue arose over Einstein's national origin. Both the Germans and the Swiss claimed him as a citizen. Since Einstein was unable to attend the Nobel ceremonies, the German ambassador officially received the prize on Einstein's behalf, and the Swiss ambassador officially awarded it to him when he returned from abroad. But the issue of Einstein's citizenship was still unsettled. The Germans said Einstein had become a German citizen when he took the job in Berlin, but Einstein took the job because Max Planck promised him he would not

need to become a German citizen. The issue was finally settled on February 7, 1924, when Einstein himself decided to accept German citizenship. Essentially, the Nobel Prize settled two issues, his citizenship and the divorce agreement with Mileva, who received the money from the prize.

Misconceptions and Myths

Most of the world in the early 1920s praised Einstein's work and admired him. C.P. Snow explained: "It seemed that, perhaps as a release from the war, people wanted a human being to revere. It is true that they did not understand what they were revering. Never mind, they believed that here was someone of supreme, if mysterious, excellence."[48] Consequently, Einstein developed the reputation close to that of a holy man who could speak wisdom. He drew huge crowds, the size usually gathered for movie stars and sports champions, not for scientists. In California, Einstein met Charlie Chaplin, and the two of them attended a celebration opening one of Chaplin's films. Crowds pushed close to the limousine to see the two celebrities. Einstein, who was bewildered, asked what it meant. Chaplin, a film star used to such attention, told him, "Nothing."

Along with the attention came misinterpretations of his theories. Trained physicists had trouble comprehending general relativity; the general public gave it humorous misinterpretations. A myth spread that only a half-dozen scientists in the world could comprehend the general theory, a condition that may have been true for a few weeks until scientists had had a chance to study it. Nevertheless,

A Physicist's Joke About Einstein's Fame

British physicist A. A. Robb, who had studied Einstein's relativity theories carefully, wrote a "Hymn to Einstein," to be sung to the tune of the German song, "Deutschland Über Alles." Ronald W. Clark *records the song in* Einstein: The Life and Times:

Scientists so unbelieving
Have completely changed their ways;
Now they humbly sing to Einstein
Everlasting hymns of praise.
Journalists in search of copy
First request an interview;
Then they boost him, boost him, boost him;
Boost him until all is blue.

He the universe created;
Spoke the word and it was there.
Now he reigns in radiant glory
On his professorial chair.
Editions of daily papers,
Yellow red and every hue
Boost him, boost him, boost him, boost him;
Boost him until all is blue.

Philosophic speculators
Stand in awe around his throne.
University professors
Blow upon his loud trombone.
Praise him on the Riemann symbols
On Christoffel symbols too
They boost him, boost him, boost him;
Boost him until all is blue.

Other scientists neglected
May be feeling somewhat sick;
And imagine that the butter
Is laid on a trifle thick.
Heed not such considerations
Be they false, or be they true;
Boost him, boost him, boost him, boost him;
Boost him until all is blue.

Einstein speaks to a small group of nonscientists about physics. His public lectures were popular but usually uncomprehended.

"Einstein" and "relativity" became synonyms for "incomprehensibility," a myth that still prevails, regardless of the number of times the theory has been explained.

Much of the misunderstanding about the theory developed because people thought "relativity" meant "relativism." To be relative means to deny firm, or absolute, standards. For example, a New York passenger asked a conductor how far it was to Central Park. The conductor told the passenger that according to Einstein, that is a relative question; it depends on how soon you need to get there. Another story tells of a physicist who stopped at an inn in a small town in Bohemia. The conversation led to physics and Einstein, and one guest said:

> These Einsteinian theories are not new in our town. They were known here long before Einstein. For twenty years our municipal doctor used to come to this inn, light his pipe, and take his first drink of beer with the words: "All is relative." Einstein did not say more.[49]

Many stories accumulated as the Einstein legend grew. For example, a New York insurance agent explained that in his office whenever people wanted to say that something was difficult, they simply said, "That is Einstein." Phillip Frank told a similar tale. While attending a lecture on Einstein's theory, he met a Catholic bishop. Told that Frank was a physicist, he said in an amazed way, "Oh, . . . are physicists also interested in Einstein's theory?" Frank also told the story about tourists in Berlin who put a lecture by Einstein on their list of sights along with the Brandenburg Gate, statues, and theatrical productions. When Einstein's lecture hall was full, he spoke for a few minutes and then paused and said, "Now I shall stop for a few minutes so that all those who have no further interest can leave." Most people then left, and Einstein lectured to the eight or ten students who remained, without being disturbed by "the sight of faces devoid of all understanding."[50]

The public seemed to think that if Einstein could prove that light did not go straight, then he could accomplish anything. Anton Reiser described the letters Einstein received:

> Poor people beg for money, for clothing, and jobs. A young man has taken the notion to become an explorer; won't Einstein help him to get to India or Africa? A woman telegraphs would the professor please obtain a visa. Actors ask for engagements; young people in small towns who have hardly attended high school would like to come to Berlin and become his disciples. . . . In addition, there come the fools and prophets, who sprout like mushrooms, especially in years of insecurity and anarchy. This one writes that he finally discovered the essence of sleep. That one writes that he has found the only correct way to lower the price of coal. Another one has invented new senses, since the old five senses are no longer sufficient for man's uses. Technicians report on their new inventions. They send blueprints of new contraptions and flying machines. Still another is engaged in overthrowing the traditional astronomy. . . . All these piles of patient paper that fools and wise men, good and bad men, have written upon pass through Einstein's hands, and not but one is read.[51]

For Einstein fame was sometimes over-whelming. He asked what all those people wanted of him and why he was not permitted to live like anyone else.

Einstein's Devotion to Zionism

On occasion Einstein fantasized a life of solitude devoted entirely to physics, but most of the time he accepted the reality of his fame and used it to influence important causes. As a Jew he felt responsible to help the Zionists. The first Zionist Congress was held in Basel, Switzerland, in 1897. It met to establish a homeland in Palestine, later called Israel, where Jews would be safe and protected by public law. Zionism became important to Einstein because he had seen prejudice against Jewish students and because of the threats on his life after 1919. Einstein continued to help the Zionists for many years because the Hebrew University in Jerusalem was important to him, yet he had reservations about the creation of Israel as a political state. He realized that a Jewish state in Palestine would displace Palestinians, who, he thought, should be left alone to live their lives.

Pacifism

Einstein continued to write and speak publicly on pacifism and internationalism after he had made the decision to stay in Germany and fight against nationalism. Einstein's *Ideas and Opinions*, his collected short articles, speeches, and letters, contains a section of thirty-five pieces on politics, government, and pacifism. Though he had first chided his colleagues during World War I for working on war projects, he recalled the manifesto he had circulated, and this time he attacked them using harsh language. Moreover, he referred to World War I events as "war crimes," instead of battles. Further, he supported student disarmament groups and conscientious objectors, men who refused to join the military on moral grounds. Einstein attended the meetings of these groups and urged total rejection of war and an economic boycott against any country that engaged in warlike activities.

In his campaign for pacifism, Einstein spoke in increasingly harsh language against militarism, a practice he had hated since the military parades in Munich and a topic that reappeared regularly throughout his life. In an essay published first in 1931, but written earlier, "The World as I See It," he said that militarism makes men act like a herd, with dull thoughts and dull feelings. He said:

This topic brings me to the worst outcrop of herd life, the military system which I abhor. That a man can take pleasure in marching in fours to the strains of a band is enough to make me despise him. He has only been given his big brain by mistake; unprotected spinal marrow was all he needed. This plague-spot of civilization ought to be abolished with all possible speed. Heroism on command, senseless violence, and all the loathsome nonsense that goes by the name of patriotism—how passionately I hate them. How vile and despicable seems war to me! I would rather be hacked

The Einsteins arrive in the United States in 1921. They are accompanied by leaders of the Zionist movement, with which Einstein sympathized.

The opening session of the League of Nations took place in Geneva, Switzerland, November 15, 1920. Einstein and fellow scientists Hendrik Lorentz and Marie Curie lent their names to this attempt to establish a world government.

in pieces than take part in such an abominable business. My opinion of the human race is high enough that I believe this bogey would have disappeared long ago, had the sound sense of people not been systematically corrupted by commercial and political interests acting through schools and the Press.[52]

Einstein's outspoken statements about war and militarism antagonized patriotic Germans, who thought he was politically unreliable. Many thought he belonged to a suspicious political party that was planning a revolution. But his feelings were his own, and he never belonged to a revolutionary party.

Internationalism

Einstein spoke as vigorously in favor of internationalism as he did for pacifism and against militarism. He approached his opinion about the wisdom of world government with the same step-by-step logic that he used in his scientific theories. Einstein reasoned that a nation developed a strong military only if its people had strong patriotic feelings. Patriotism led citizens to desire wealth and power for their nation. The result was war, a cruel waste. Much better, Einstein thought, would be a world government to oversee cooperation

The League of Nations

In their history, Civilization: Past and Present, *T. Walter Wallbank and Alastair M. Taylor describe the purposes of the League of Nations:*

"In 1920, it was the first time in history that a carefully planned scheme for the encouragement of international cooperation had been established. Following the Great War the world stood in dire need of such an agency. Misery and confusion were prevalent in Europe. In Poland the peasants were faced with famine, in Russia typhus and cholera stalked through the land, and even the victorious French were faced with the immense task of restoring their devastated regions. At one time more than seventy-five million people were dependent on supplies given by the Allies, mainly the United States! The political scene also reflected chaos. . . .

The postwar world, especially Europe, obviously presented serious problems. But it was generally felt that political anarchy and economic confusion rife in certain areas of the globe would gradually be removed by the constructive efforts of the League of Nations. Before tracing the achievements and failures of the League in the decade following the Great War it will be useful to see just how the framers of the League intended it to operate as an agency of international reconstruction. Its purposes may be thought of as fourfold: (1) to prevent war and punish aggression, (2) to organize peace, (3) to assume certain duties connected with the operation of the peace treaties, and (4) to stimulate international cooperation for the removal of economic and social evils and for general humanitarian and cultural purposes."

and to prevent fights among nations. After the devastation of World War I, many people took up the idea of getting nations to live together in peace.

In the spring of 1919, a man named Sir Eric Drummond received $500,000 to employ a staff and build a world government. He established a headquarters in Geneva, Switzerland, to build the League of Nations. Einstein received an invitation to work on the committee to carry out this plan, as did his friend Hendrik Lorentz from the Netherlands and Marie Curie, a scientist from France. Einstein joined the committee in May 1922, but he resigned and rejoined three times between 1922

In the 1920s Einstein's life was filled with interviews, lecturing, traveling, and promoting political causes. Here, he and Elsa are met by Lord Haldane as they arrive at Cambridge University for a lecture in 1921.

and 1931. Because Einstein was outspoken and found it hard to compromise, he was a poor committee member, but the group needed his presence because his fame lent support to the cause. Einstein believed in the concept of world government even though he felt ambivalent about committee work and his fitness for the task. Though he attended meetings only part of the time, he spoke and wrote for world government and supported the League of Nations whenever he could.

During the decade of the 1920s, interviews, lectures, travel, and causes took much of Einstein's attention. Nevertheless, he still had time for a personal life, his work, and a fiftieth birthday before the Nazis and Hitler rose to power and began systematic persecution of the Jews.

Chapter

6 Quiet Life, the Rise of Hitler, and Departure from Berlin: 1920-1933

After the whirl of travels and lectures, Einstein settled in at 5 Haberlandstrasse, his apartment in Berlin where he enjoyed physics, music, and friends. At home he worked in a small turret, a tower built to ornament the building. It had two little rooms, furnished simply with an old armchair and a desk. On the wall hung pictures of three men Einstein admired—scientists Michael Faraday and James Maxwell and philosopher Arthur Schopenhauer. In that room he sat, or walked, and thought, needing nothing more than a pen, a pad of paper, and his mind. Elsa allowed no visitors into the turret, only his assistants and his secretary. Elsa made time for Einstein to play his violin daily and invited friends and occasionally a professional musician to play Mozart and Bach with him. Einstein's interests

Einstein playing the violin. Einstein's wife, Elsa, made sure he had time in his busy schedule to join friends for music making.

Help for a Lonely Student

In an essay entitled "To Albert Einstein on his 75th Birthday," Leopold Infeld recalls his first meeting with Einstein when he was a lonely student in Berlin. Einstein treated Infeld kindly, and Infeld never forgot. The essay is published in Einstein: The First Hundred Years:

"I saw Einstein for the first time in Berlin in 1921, when I was pacing the streets, trying my best to become a student at the university where Planck, Laue and Einstein lectured. I felt unhappy, because I knew nobody. I was lonely, as one can feel lonely only in a great hostile city. For weeks I waited for appointments with people—only to find how little they cared whether or not I was accepted by the University of Berlin. Yet at that time this seemed to me the decisive question of my life. In desperation I rang up Einstein and, to my great astonishment, was asked to come right over.

Kindness is a difficult thing to take when it comes, suddenly against an icy background of hostility and indifference. Einstein greeted me with a smile and offered me a cigarette, talked to me as an equal and showed a childlike trust in everything I said. My short interview was an important event in my life. Instead of thinking about his genius, about his achievements in physics, I thought then and later about his great kindness, about his loud laughs, about the gentle way he talked, about the brilliance of his eyes, about the clumsiness with which he looked for a piece of paper on a desk full of papers, about the queer mixture of great warmth and great aloofness."

included philosophy and literature as well as music and all the sciences. He liked friends and guests such as artists, philosophers, as well as physicists whose conversation involved questions and thoughts and ideas. Einstein also liked his little sailboat, which he used on the lakes around Berlin. Alone in his boat, he absorbed the quiet beauty of the lake and let his thoughts turn to the universe and its laws.

Einstein's Distaste for Hypocrisy and Pretension

In spite of his newfound fame, Einstein continued to despise social pretension and professional hypocrisy. He worked in casual pants and a sweater; he lectured in a sports suit and sandals. At one formal party Elsa pointed out to Albert that he had forgotten his socks. When he had no dress suit for a formal lecture in Oslo, Norway, Einstein put on his usual dinner jacket and volunteered to pin a tag on it that said "This suit has just been brushed."[53] Einstein was not merely careless; he believed that dressing up reflected false striving for quality and class and covered up the true self. Similarly, he disapproved of students and colleagues who took easy questions and tried to make trivial scientific studies look complicated. He knew one physicist who took the easy way and said about him, "He strikes me as a man who looks for the thinnest spot in a board and then bores as many holes as possible through it."[54] He liked scholars who took hard problems even if they could never quite solve them. Consequently, he had only a few students for whom he was the official advisor, since the problems Einstein approved were too difficult for most students. Yet Einstein liked working with young people in an informal way because they had sincere enthusiasm and sincere ideals. In his modest and friendly way, he willingly listened to them and gave them his thoughts; he was the kind of teacher he would have liked as a student in Munich.

Scientific Issues: Quantum Mechanics

After 1923 Einstein gave his professional attention to three main scientific issues: the research that developed from his theories, his search for a unified field theory, and the philosophy of science. One measure of a theory's value is the amount of research that generates from it. Einstein's 1905 paper on light quanta opened up a new field in physics that came to be known as quantum mechanics, an approach to the theory of atoms.

In 1905 Einstein showed that light is both particle and wave, and he showed that atoms can be measured statistically. Based on these ideas, physicists in the 1920s studied the atom—what it is and how it works. After British physicist Ernest Rutherford had shown that an atom has a nucleus with electrons around it, Danish physicist Niels Bohr tried to show that an atom works as Newton thought gravity worked; that is, that electrons circled around the nucleus as planets circled around the sun. He found that he was wrong and formulated a new theory instead. The conclusion was that the electrons orbiting around the nu-

Danish physicist Niels Bohr's important research on atoms resulted from Einstein's theory of light.

He expressed his ideas in articles such as "A Mathematician's Mind," "The Religious Spirit of Science," "Science and Religion," "On Scientific Truth," and "Physics and Reality." He believed that a scientist must be dedicated to truth and have faith in the human ability to reason. In "Science and Religion," he said:

> But science can only be created by those who are thoroughly imbued with the aspirations toward truth and understanding. This source of feeling, however, springs from the sphere of religion. To this there also belongs the faith in the possibility that the regulations valid for the world of existence are rational, that is, comprehensible to reason. I cannot conceive of a genuine scientist without this profound faith. The situation may be expressed by an image: science without religion is lame, religion without science is blind.[56]

Einstein's Heart Ailment

In 1928 Einstein became seriously ill on a trip to Switzerland. Elsa joined friends in Zurich to take care of him for a few weeks until he was strong enough to return to Berlin. There Dr. Janos Plesh diagnosed an inflammation of the walls of the heart, put Einstein on a diet, and ordered rest. Einstein and his family moved to a small resort where Einstein rested in bed for four months and stayed quiet for the remainder of a year. He cancelled all lectures and trips, but was well enough to think and work on his theories. Actually, he found his recuperation quite pleasant, except that he now had no secretary since

he was away from Berlin. In April 1928, he hired Helen Dukas, who remained his secretary for the rest of his life.

Einstein at Fifty

On March 14, 1929, Einstein turned fifty, and the day became another world event. To escape reporters, Einstein hid in the gardener's cottage at Dr. Plesh's lake home and kept his whereabouts a secret. Only his family celebrated with him. Enough birthday cards came from physicists, philosophers, pacifists, Zionists, and ordinary people to fill several wash baskets. He received a sailboat from a Berlin bank, a plot of land in Palestine with trees

Albert's secretary Helen Dukas (left) and Elsa Einstein. Dukas, hired in 1928 while Einstein recuperated from heart trouble, remained his secretary for the rest of his life.

Einstein posing in the new sailboat he received on his fiftieth birthday. Sailing afforded him much coveted solitude.

planted on it to be named "Einstein's Grove," and a small package of tobacco from an unemployed man who had saved nickels to buy the present. His note apologized for the small amount, but assured Einstein that the quality was good. Einstein answered his note first.

The Berlin city officials wanted to give Einstein a house, but their present turned into a fiasco. First, they gave him a house on public property, but people lived in it and had a lease to stay there. Next, they tried to build on another site nearby, but the lease prevented any buildings on that location. Then, they chose a third site, only to discover that the city did not own it. Finally, Elsa chose a plot near a lake in Caputh, a village outside Berlin, but building was postponed. By that time Einstein's birthday was long past and he wrote to the mayor:

My dear Mr. Mayor: Human life is very short, while the authorities work very slowly. I feel therefore that my life is too short for me to adapt myself to your methods. I thank you for your friendly intentions. Now, however, my birthday is already past and I decline the gift."[57]

The Einsteins liked the location in Caputh so much that they bought it themselves and built their own house, but the project cost them their entire savings. Nonetheless, they liked the summer house with the nearby lake and woods and entertained many visitors there.

Rise of Nazism and Hitler

When the Einsteins settled into their house in Caputh, the political situation in Germany was developing in ways that soon

Adolf Hitler's rise to power in Germany in 1933 made the Nazis the ruling party in Germany. The Nazis' violent hatred of Jews drove Albert Einstein from Germany to the United States.

World War I Treaty of Versailles, and the idea that the German army had not been defeated, but rather had been betrayed by pacifists and Jews who had refused to help with the war.

Winter in California

Shortly after 1929, Einstein received an offer from the California Institute of Technology at Pasadena to visit and lecture. Einstein was particularly interested in the California offer because new, powerful telescopes had recently become available for cosmology and because he wanted to meet Edwin Hubble, who had verified a prediction in general relativity. He agreed to go to America for a winter term in 1931. Even before Einstein left Germany, American companies offered him money to endorse cleaning disinfectants, toilet waters, clothes, and musical instruments, offers not in keeping with Einstein's taste. His arrival in 1931 outdid his arrival a decade earlier, as Ronald Clark described:

disrupted the lives of the Einsteins and all the Jews in the country. The Nazis rose to power under Adolf Hitler's leadership. Hitler rose to power on a campaign of hate. His themes included attacks on Jews and Communists, the injustice of the

Einstein, chalk in hand, stops in mid-equation to pose with other scientists at Cal Tech in Pasadena in 1931. Famed astronomer Edwin Hubble is second from left.

Einstein comments on a particular feature of a model of the new, giant telescope then being built for the Mount Wilson Observatory near Pasadena.

The occasion, when it came, had an air of comedy. Fifty reporters and fifty photographers swooped on their victim. Einstein, good natured but bewildered, was called upon "within the brief quarter of an hour to define the fourth dimension in one word, state his theory of relativity in one sentence, give his views on prohibition, comment on politics and religion, and discuss the virtues of his violin." The German consul, Paul Schwarz, helped interpret; Elsa did her best to stage-manage the occasion, mothering her husband away from the trick questions, explaining, and sympathizing with those who wanted the theory of relativity described in a few one-syllable words.[58]

After a round of tours, the Einsteins went on to Pasadena, where Einstein visited the Mount Wilson Observatory and met Edwin Hubble.

Einstein Leaves Germany Forever

For three years Einstein spent the winter term in Pasadena and the fall term at Christ Church College in Oxford, England. When Einstein left Caputh in the fall of 1932 for his third winter in California, he told Elsa to look carefully at their villa before leaving because, he said, they would never see it again. While they were in America, Hitler was voted into office on January 30, 1933. Before sailing from New York to return to Europe, Einstein spoke publicly about the dangers of Hitler. As he left, German consul Schwarz unofficially informed Einstein that returning to Germany would be too dangerous. When the Einsteins arrived in Belgium, they went to an obscure coastal village. In March and April, Einstein resigned from the Berlin Academy, renounced his German citizenship, turned in his German passport, and withdrew from the Bavarian Academy. His letter to the Berlin Academy said, "I do not wish to live in a country where the individual does not enjoy equality before the law, and freedom of speech and teaching."[59] The Berlin newspaper headline read, "Good News from Einstein—

Einstein in front of the country house at Caputh. In 1932, when he and Elsa left Caputh for their annual winter trip to England and America, he knew they would never return.

The Sweep of Nazi Control

Historians T. Walter Wallbank and Alastair M. Taylor in Civilization: Past and Present *describe the widespread effect of Hitler's purge and power:*

"Assisted by such lieutenants as Goering, Goebbels, Himmler (head of the dread Gestapo, or secret police), Hess, and Von Ribbentrop, Hitler now ruthlessly smashed and uprooted the democratic institutions by which he was brought to power. . . .

In domestic affairs Hitler ruthlessly put into practice his ideas of racial superiority. A national boycott against the Jews was proclaimed in April 1933, and they were barred from public service. Discrimination of all sorts followed. Many noted scholars either were sent to concentration camps or fled the country. Among those fortunate enough to escape were such Nobel prize winners as Albert Einstein and James Franck, physicists, and Fritz Haber, the chemist.

Hitler was not content with racial discrimination alone. All labor unions were disbanded. . . . Since Nazi doctrine elevated the state above all else, a movement was instigated to subordinate religion to the Hitler regime. . . .

Joseph Goebbels, Hitler's minister of propaganda.

Education and public opinion were coordinated for Nazi needs. A Reich culture cabinet was set up to control literature, the press, broadcasting, drama, music, art, and the cinema. All of these agencies were to reflect only one attitude, one pattern of thought, and one stream of esthetic appreciation. Goebbels was given the task of controlling the minds and hearts of the German people with his department of propaganda. From this department broadcasting stations sent programs abroad, jamming the air lanes to disrupt the broadcasts of other nations. Goebbels also provided radio fare for the German listener and spied on the people to see whether they listened to forbidden foreign broadcasts.

Einstein awaits his turn to speak at a 1933 symposium in England's Royal Albert Hall. He was again a man without a country.

He's Not Coming Back."[60] Once again Einstein had given up his German citizenship, but now he was also without a home.

Hitler's Purges

On April 1, 1933, Hitler began to purge Germany of Jews. Hitler's officers seized Einstein's bank account and all securities, closed and locked his apartment on Haberlandstrasse, seized his house in Caputh, published a book which listed one hundred professors against Einstein, offered a $5,000 reward to the person who would kill Einstein, and denounced his relativity theory in the Nazi newspaper. The May issue of the Nazi newspaper *Volkische Boebachter* published an article written by Philip Lenard, in which he said:

> The most important example of the dangerous influence of the Jewish circles on the study of nature has been provided by Herr Einstein with his mathematically botched-up theories consisting of some ancient knowledge and a few arbitrary additions. This theory now gradually falls to pieces, as is the fate of all products that are estranged from nature. Even scientists who have otherwise done solid work cannot escape the reproach that they allowed the relativity theory to get a foothold in Germany, because they did not see, or did not want to see, how wrong it is, outside the field of science also, to regard this Jew as a good German.[61]

On April 12, Einstein's stepdaughters, his assistant, and his doctor left for France and got out safely. Hitler's attack on Einstein, however, was only a beginning. Hitler dismissed scores of Jewish professors from German universities. On May 10, forty thousand people cheered as they

German rabbis are herded together during Hitler's roundup of Jews in the 1930s. Einstein's family had escaped the Nazi purge.

watched a pile of two thousand books burn. And the Nazis planned extermination programs for non-Aryans, the name for Jews.

The summer of 1933 was a chaotic time for Einstein as he tried to find a safe hiding place, decide where to make a new home, and carry out his fall lectures at Christ Church College, Oxford. He and Elsa hid in England in a remote village before going to Oxford. He had offers for jobs in England, Belgium, Spain, France, Jerusalem, and Pasadena, California. In a letter to his friend Solovine, he said he had more offers for professorial chairs than he had reasonable ideas in his head.

While at Oxford he received an offer from the newly formed Institute for Advanced Study in Princeton, New Jersey, an offer proposed to him while he was still in Caputh. In the discussion concerning salary, Einstein thought he needed $3,000 a year unless he found he could live on less. Abraham Flexner, who was setting up the institute, was shocked at the small request, spoke to Elsa, and decided on a salary of $16,000. On October 7, 1933, Einstein left Southampton, England, for America with Elsa, Dr. Meyer, his assistant, and Helen Dukas, his secretary. He was sailing to a new home.

7 America and the Institute for Advanced Study: 1933-1945

Einstein arrived in America with none of the hoopla characteristic of his previous arrivals at New York Harbor. Two trustees of the Institute for Advanced Study had arranged for a tugboat to take Einstein and his small party off the ship before it docked. They were then driven quietly to Princeton, where a temporary home had been rented for him. Einstein arrived, changed his clothes, and walked out alone into the Princeton streets to explore. On Nassau Street he stopped at an ice-cream parlor, the Baltimore, and bought an ice-cream cone. Princeton Seminary student John Lampe, in the Baltimore at the time, described Einstein's first experience as an American resident:

> Yet Einstein walked through the doorway just as the waitress behind the counter handed me my special ice-cream cone! The great man looked at the cone, smiled at me, turned to the girl, and pointed his thumb first at the cone and then at himself.
>
> I wish I could say that I had the generosity or presence of mind to pay for Einstein's first typically American treat. But that would not be the truth. When the waitress handed his cone over the counter, Einstein gave her a coin and she made change, muttering something like, "This one goes in my memory book."
>
> Einstein and I stood there together, then nibbling our ice-cream cones and looking out the window into Nassau Street. Neither of us said anything. We finished the cones about the same instant and I think I held the door for him as he stepped out.[62]

The incident turned out to be typical of life for Einstein in Princeton, whose residents accepted him without bothering him and where he walked the streets alone.

Einstein in Princeton

Princeton, New Jersey, home of Princeton University, had hills and woods, well-kept houses, and elegant gray-stone university buildings. After a year or two in the rented house, the Einsteins bought a home at 112 Mercer Street, an old, two-story house with a big garden. Einstein built a study on the second floor, replacing half of a wall with windows for a garden view. There he had his books and portraits of Faraday, Maxwell, and Gandhi, an Indian pacifist. They used their old furniture, which the Nazis had sent from their Berlin apartment at 5 Haberlandstrasse.

The Einsteins bought this modest home in Princeton just a few minutes' walk from the Princeton University campus.

Life in a New Country

From the time of his arrival as an American resident, Einstein received an enormous number of invitations to be a guest of honor. Elsa helped to screen some of the requests, and Abraham Flexner, the head of the Institute for Advanced Study, screened or arranged others. Ronald W. Clark identifies a few of them:

> Einstein made his American debut as a violinist at a public concert, attended as guest of honor a dinner given by Governor Lehmann, was officially welcomed as a resident of New Jersey, and attended public celebrations to set the first type for an enlarged edition of the *Jewish Daily Bulletin*, all within a few months of his arrival.[63]

In November President Franklin Roosevelt invited the Einsteins to visit the White House, but they never received the invitation. At first Einstein's secretary accepted the invitation for Einstein, but Flexner intervened and called the president's secretary, telling him that Einstein had come to Princeton to do scientific work in seclusion and the visit would be too public. In a follow-up letter, Flexner implied that he had declined the invitation with Einstein's desire and consent. Einstein learned of the invitation in a letter from a different White House staff member who casually mentioned Einstein's refusal of the president's invitation. Einstein wrote to Mrs. Roosevelt saying that no invitation had reached him, but he would be very interested in meeting the president. He regretted the mistake and wanted "to avoid the ugly impression that I had been negligent or discourteous in this matter."[64] The Einsteins received a second invitation and visited the White House in January, a visit Einstein especially enjoyed because President Roosevelt spoke German.

Although Elsa wanted to join the social life in Princeton, Einstein avoided the dinners and receptions given by the faculty, as he had in Berlin. They entertained visitors from town, scientists who came to see Einstein, refugees from Germany, Zionists, writers, journalists, and artists. Stories circulated about the ten-year-old girl who visited Einstein for help with her arithmetic because he explained it so that she understood. And a Princeton busdriver thought Einstein was bad at arithmetic because he

Eleanor and President Franklin Roosevelt. The Einsteins were invited to meet the Roosevelts in January 1934. The president's ability to speak German delighted Einstein.

had trouble with change. There was the day Einstein called the institute's office for his address because he was out walking and had forgotten how to get back home. He developed a reputation in the town as a kind and quiet, but forgetful, man.

Out of all the countries Einstein could have chosen for his new home, he chose America for its promising intellectual climate. During the 1920s and 1930s America awarded many doctoral degrees in physics, sent many scientists to study in European centers, sponsored European scientists to visit and lecture in American universities, and provided grant money for small projects and new equipment. According to Gerald Holton, America already had a high level of accomplishment in science when the purge in Germany, Austria, and Italy "provided the necessary critical infusion of high talent that helped to turn the United States into the world's preeminent country for the pursuit of frontier research."[65] Einstein stressed the open-minded attitude and the high energy of American scientists.

Einstein's New Job

In this favorable climate Einstein found an especially suitable job. Two wealthy Americans, Mr. Louis Bamberger and Mrs. Felix Fuld, had provided money to gather scholars in mathematical science to do research and discuss their projects with one another. They hired Flexner to direct the establishment of an institute and select the scholars, whose only obligation was to do their research projects at the institute between October and April. In the fall of 1933, the institute had quarters in the

Three Physics Problems

Einstein had three physics problems to work on. First, he wanted to find field equations and be able to derive the laws of motion from them. Second, he wanted to develop the quantum theory. And, third, he wanted to find a unified theory that would combine equations of the electromagnetic and gravitational fields. Elsa explained to friends that Einstein worked very hard during this period, putting in long hours sometimes far into the night. Einstein had worked for many years on the unified theory and had published a number of papers on it. Because of his popularity, the public anticipated a new discovery, another breakthrough in the riddle of the universe. Windows along New York's Fifth

While at Princeton, Einstein worked long and hard on three physics problems: quantum theory, a unified field theory, and a new way to express the laws of motion.

Abraham Flexner was appointed head of Princeton University's newly established Institute for Advanced Study. He is credited with persuading Einstein to come to Princeton.

mathematics department at Princeton University until the new building was built in 1940. Carved into the wall of the new institute building are Einstein's words: "God is sophisticated, but he is not malicious." The institute job appealed to Einstein because he could work with seventeen outstanding scientists, and he would have no interruptions from undergraduate students. After a time, however, he missed students. Young people began seeking his advice, and he gave each one his attention. He watched their progress, advised them about instructors, suggested what books to read, and even sent them books himself.

(Left) Dr. Hans Albert Einstein, Einstein's eldest son and a professor in Zurich, Switzerland, visited his father at Princeton in 1937. (Right) Leopold Infeld, befriended by Einstein in Berlin, sought his help in coming to America. He later became a University of Toronto physics professor.

Avenue displayed equations from his work, and curious crowds stopped to look at them, but no new breakthrough occurred. When asked if the failure to achieve his goal depressed him, Einstein said no because he learned from the failures, that he knew at least ninety-nine ways the equations did not work. And he kept trying to find one that did.

Family and Refugees

By the summer of 1934, Einstein still had three years left in his contract to give fall lectures at Christ Church College, Oxford. He cancelled this appointment and urged that the money allotted for his salary be used to help refugee professors from Germany. Instead of going to England, Einstein spent the summer at the seaside cottage of Dr. Bucky, a friend the Einsteins had known in Leipzig. There he spent the summer sailing with Bucky and his family. The 1934 summer of sailing began an activity which he pursued every summer for many years. Elsa left in May for Paris to be with her daughter Ilse, who was seriously ill, and her other daughter Margot, who was caring for her sister. Ilse died soon after Elsa arrived, and she returned to America. Within a short time other family members came to America. Elsa's daughter Margot and her husband and Ilse's husband Rudolf Kayser arrived first. Soon after, Einstein's older son Hans Albert came, and two years later Einstein's sister Maja came from Italy.

As the Germans continued to persecute the Jews, many Jews sought refuge in America and asked Einstein for help. He used his influence whenever he could to help refugees find jobs. For example, the young violinist Boris Swartz and his father, who had visited Einstein in Berlin, managed to get to America. Einstein persuaded conductor Eugene Ormandy to help them find opportunities to play in concerts. Einstein got Leopold Infeld, the student he befriended in Berlin, a one-year job as his assistant and collaborated with him on a science book when the assistantship ran out.

Requests for Einstein's Words

In addition, there were other requests for his time and attention. Newspapers and periodicals wanted him to write articles and meet reporters for interviews, charities asked him to make appearances at fund-raisers, and Zionists wanted Einstein to endorse their cause. Einstein used these opportunities to speak for the social and moral ideas he felt strongly about. A sampling from his collected short papers and speeches illustrate the range of his opinions and the eloquence and humor with which he spoke on them. Invited to write a message for a Time Capsule at the New York World's Fair, he wrote, "Dear Posterity, If you have not become more just, more peaceful, and generally more rational than we are—why then, the Devil take you." Einstein also spoke out against racism in America. He wrote an article telling Americans that "men of good will" must have courage to combat racism by "word and deed." In another article he wrote about science and ethics; he said, "It is the privilege of man's moral genius . . . to advance ethical axioms which are so comprehensive and so well founded that men will accept them. . . . Truth is what stands the test of experience."

In response to a political threat to limit professors' freedom to speak and to teach, he told a gathering, "Let all of us therefore summon our strength. Let us be tirelessly on guard lest it be said later of the intellectual elite of this land: Timidly and without a struggle they surrendered a heritage handed down to them by their forefathers—a heritage of which they were not worthy."[66] The same themes, important to him since childhood, thread their way through all Einstein's words: justice, freedom, moral courage, and human decency.

Elsa's Illness and Death

Not many months after the Einsteins moved into their house on Mercer Street, Elsa became very ill with a heart and kidney ailment. Doctors recommended bed rest for nearly two months. Though weakened, she recovered enough to spend the summer with Einstein at a lake in upstate New York. Her illness occurred at a time when Einstein was particularly engrossed in his work. Elsa confided to a friend that her husband was a wonderful man, but being his wife was difficult. When she needed sympathy and tenderness, he was absorbed in his physics. At the end of the summer, they returned to Mercer Street, and Elsa lived until December 21. Filled with grief, Einstein found that he was unable to concentrate. But he had known sadness before and had found that continued efforts in his work helped him recover from his sorrow.

After Elsa's death, Einstein lived on at 112 Mercer Street. His stepdaughter Margot, divorced from her husband, came to live there too. Then, Helen Dukas became Einstein's housekeeper as well as his secretary, and managed his life much as Elsa had. In 1939 Einstein's sister Maja came to America for a visit, but she never went

The Joy of Sailing

Sailing was Einstein's favorite sport from the time he was a student in Zurich. In Albert Einstein: A Biographical Portrait, *Anton Reiser describes the joy Einstein derived from sailing in his later years:*

"Einstein is not interested in long trips of speed records. He is interested in daydreams. He enjoys the distant views, the light, the colors, the quiet shores and the soothing, gliding motion of the boat, steered by a slight motion of the rudder. All this creates within him a happy feeling of freedom. His scientific thinking, which never leaves him even on the water, takes on the nature of a daydream. Theoretical thinking is rich in imagination; without imagination no reality can be attained. While his hand grasps the rudder, Einstein takes delight in explaining to his companions his latest scientific ideas, and in the summery atmosphere the abstract thought processes become so permeated with the processes of the scientist's deepest emotion that one realizes the unity in him of a free existence and ever-dominating work. He handles the boat with the skill and fearlessness of a boy. He raises the sails himself, climbs around the boat in order to straighten out ropes and lines, and works poles and hooks to cast the ship off from shore. The joy of this activity is reflected in his face, in his words, in his happy laughter."

Einstein on his sailboat.

back, and she joined the household. For several years Einstein lived in his house with these three women. By late 1935 when Einstein realized he would never return to Europe, he sought American citizenship. He, Margot, and Helen applied and, after the appropriate waiting period, took the exams. On October 1, 1940, they were sworn in as American citizens. Maja never became a citizen.

New Views on Pacifism

In the last years of the 1930s, Einstein struggled with his views on pacifism, which he had begun to question before he moved to America. Hitler's purge of Jews and dissidents—eventually murdering 2.5 million, dismissing hundreds from jobs, and driving many from their homeland—made Einstein realize the need to fight Hitler. He thought that perhaps the pacifists in France and England had created a vacuum of power that had allowed Hitler to believe he could gain control. Ronald W. Clark explained the reason for the change in Einstein's view:

> Events had taught him, in the words of his friend Max Born, "that the ultimate ethical values, on which all human existence is based, must, as a last resort, be defended even by force and with the sacrifice of human lives.". . . Circumstances altered cases; even in pacifism there were no absolutes. The war had to be won.[67]

Einstein saw that he had no good choices in his dilemma: either choose pacifism and allow Hitler's evil power to prevail or use force and violence to stop Hitler's evil power. Einstein had decided that the second was the better, if more terrible, choice.

Complicating Einstein's dilemma was the knowledge that he had developed the theory that made the building of an atomic bomb possible. Einstein's 1907 paper developed the equation $E=mc^2$, a discovery showing that a small amount of mass can release a huge amount of energy. Shortly after publication, a physicist spoke privately with him to ask him if the theory could be used to make a weapon. Einstein dismissed him immediately.

Development of Atomic Fission

Before a weapon could be made, scientists first had to find a mass, an atom, that could be split in order to release energy. At

Einstein, his stepdaughter Margot (right), and Helen Dukas, his secretary and housekeeper (far right), take their oaths as American citizens on October 1, 1940.

one time when asked about splitting the atom, Einstein said, "Splitting the atom by bombardment is like shooting at birds in the dark in a region where there are few birds."[68] But Leo Szilard, who had been with Einstein in Berlin, thought the task would not be that difficult. Then scientists discovered that the uranium atom could be split.

During 1938 and 1939 events relating to splitting the atom happened quickly. At the end of 1938 German physicist Otto Hahn had split the nucleus of the uranium atom in two, an action called fission. He sent the results of his research to physicist Lise Meitner in Sweden, and she studied them with her nephew Otto Frisch, who worked in Niels Bohr's Copenhagen Institute. They immediately telephoned Bohr, who was soon to leave for America to attend the Fifth Washington Conference on Theoretical Physics. Bohr announced the discovery to the physicists gathered at the conference.

Only a few weeks later in Paris, a team of researchers led by Frederic Joliot-Curie, son-in-law of Marie Curie, confirmed that fission (breaking apart) of the uranium nucleus set loose neutrons, which could bombard the nucleus of other uranium atoms and thus set off a chain reaction. The team applied for a patent to make a uranium bomb. In America, physicists Leo Szilard and Enrico Fermi duplicated and confirmed both Hahn's and Joliot-Curie's experiments.

In April 1939, two German physicists recommended that the German War Office investigate nuclear explosives. Soon after, two German projects were underway. In the meanwhile Belgium ordered fifty tons of uranium ore, and England worked to secure its own supply of uranium and worked to find ways of keeping large quantities of uranium from Germany. Fermi and Szilard recognized the need to keep uranium from the Germans and the need for the American military to be informed. Einstein, they thought, might be able to help.

Warning to President Roosevelt

Einstein was spending the summer at a cottage on Long Island when Szilard went to see him. Since Einstein and the queen of Belgium were friends, Szilard had planned for Einstein to request that she use her influence to see that the Germans bought none of the uranium mined at the Belgium-owned mine in the Belgian Congo. Then Szilard thought that a letter to President Roosevelt signed by Einstein was better than a letter to the queen. Einstein listened to Szilard's ideas. Einstein knew about Otto Hahn's discovery of nuclear fission, but he had not kept up with all developments in nuclear physics while he had been busy on his own research. Although he thought chances were slight that the Germans would successfully develop a bomb, one chance in a million was too great a risk, and he felt the Americans should go ahead with research.

In a letter dated August 2, 1939, Einstein explained to the president the discoveries in nuclear fission that could lead to the development of a bomb. He suggested sources for uranium ore, recommended funding for research and development, and informed him of developments in Germany. The letter reached President Roosevelt in mid-October after the war had

Einstein Warns President Roosevelt

In his essay entitled "Einstein the Pacifist Warrior," Joseph Rotblat included a copy of Einstein's letter to President Roosevelt in 1939, giving information about an atomic bomb and making recommendations. He also included the president's reply. Rotblat's essay appears in Einstein: The First Hundred Years:

A page from Einstein's letter to FDR.

"Some recent work by E. Fermi and L. Szilard, which has been communicated to me in manuscript, leads me to expect that the element uranium may be turned into a new and important source of energy in the immediate future. Certain aspects of the situation seem to call for watchfulness and, if necessary, quick action on the part of the Administration. I believe, therefore, that it is my duty to bring to your attention the following facts and recommendations.

In the course of the last four months it has been made probable—through the work of Joliot in France as well as Fermi and Szilard in America—that it may become possible to set up nuclear chain reactions in a large mass of uranium, by which vast amounts of power and large quantities of new radium-like elements would be generated. Now it appears almost certain that this could be achieved in the immediate future.

This new phenomenon would also lead to the construction of bombs, and it is conceivable—though much less certain—that extremely powerful bombs of a new type may thus be constructed. A single bomb of this type, carried by boat or exploded in a port, might very well destroy the whole port together with some of the surrounding territory. However, such bombs might very well prove to be too heavy for transportation by air. . . .

You may think it desirable to have some permanent contact maintained between the Administration and the group of physicists working on chain reactions in America. One possible way of achieving this might be for you to entrust with this task a person who has your confidence and who could perhaps serve in an unofficial capacity."

begun in Europe. The president replied promptly, thanking Einstein for his letter and informing him that he had convened a board to investigate his suggestions.

America Makes the Bomb

Einstein was asked to work on the president's committee, which convened to make initial plans, but he declined, although he worked part-time as a consultant for the U.S. Navy's Bureau of Ordnance. The investigation went forward and later became known as the Manhattan Project, with research done in Chicago, Illinois, and Los Alamos, New Mexico. Einstein's involvement ended once the project was underway, and he went on with his own work until the closing months of the war.

By early 1945, Germany was all but defeated, but in America plans already had been made to use the bomb against Japan. Szilard thought this decision would have dangerous effects on postwar relations and might start a nuclear-arms race. Again he met with Einstein and urged him to write another letter to President Roosevelt. On March 25, 1945, Einstein wrote the letter asking him to arrange an interview for Szilard, but the letter never reached Roosevelt, who died in April.

President Truman arranged a meeting for Szilard and one of his staff, but the two could not reach an agreement. Further efforts on the part of other scientists failed as well, and two bombs dropped on Hiroshima and Nagasaki, two Japanese cities. On August 6, at a lake for the summer holiday, Einstein heard the news on the radio. To the *New York Times* reporter who came

A plume of radioactive dust rises miles into the air over Hiroshima, Japan, on August 6, 1945. Einstein's equation that had changed physics also revolutionized warfare.

to the house, Einstein said that the world was not ready for $E=mc^2$, the theory that made development of the bomb possible.

When the bombs dropped in August, Einstein was sixty-six years old and had been officially retired from the Institute for Advanced Study for four months. On August 11 the Smyth Report—*Atomic Energy for Military Purposes*—was published. This report identified Einstein as the man who revolutionized modern warfare. He was the man who had developed the theory making a bomb possible and the man who had made the attempt to write President Roosevelt. Again the quiet and humble man was in the limelight—this time for his conscience, not his theories. He spent the next ten years speaking, broadcasting, and writing, as long as his strength allowed.

8 Retirement Years: 1945-1955

In April 1945, when Einstein formally retired from the institute, he kept his study there and worked on as he had since 1933 and continued to live in his house on Mercer Street, trying, as usual, to live a quiet life. In the last decade of his life, however, he remained in the public eye as much as before.

The Einstein who had been a celebrity in the 1920s was still a popular world figure two decades later. Fame had failed to change his humble, unpretentious attitude, nor had it affected his will to speak clear and honest thoughts. The public still wanted to see, hear, and honor him. In December 1945, shortly after the end of World War II, he gave the address at the Fifth Nobel Anniversary Dinner at the Hotel Astor in New York. In plain words Einstein told his audience that "the war is won, but the peace is not; . . . the picture of our postwar world is not bright; . . . there is no escape into easy comforts; . . . the situation calls for courageous effort." [69]

In 1946 the Emergency Committee of Atomic Scientists, organized to inform Americans about atomic energy and its implications, called on Einstein to be its president. In 1946 the Hebrew University asked Einstein to join the new science institute. In 1947 the Foreign Press Association gave Einstein its annual award for promoting peaceful uses for atomic energy. In 1948 he received the One World Award and addressed an audience in Carnegie Hall in New York. He told his audience:

I am greatly touched by the signal honor which you have wished to confer on me. In the course of my long life I have received from my fellowmen far more recognition than I deserve, and I confess that my sense of shame has always outweighed my pleasure therein. But never, on any previous occasion, has the pain so far outweighed the pleasure as now. For all of us who are concerned for peace and the triumph of reason and justice must today be keenly aware how small an influence reason and honest goodwill exert upon events in the political field. [70]

Einstein at Seventy

In 1949 Einstein turned seventy, an occasion that brought fewer gifts than his fiftieth birthday but more honors. The institute celebrated his birthday with a conference at which selected scientists read papers. As a further honor, scientists named

In honor of his seventieth birthday, Einstein receives an honorary doctorate from Jerusalem's Hebrew University. The ceremony took place at his home in Princeton and was attended by officials of the Hebrew University and various American Jewish groups.

a new, artificially created element after him called einsteinium. In addition, Paul Arthur Schilpp published *Albert Einstein: Philosopher-Scientist*, a collection of essays in which scientists and philosophers discuss and evaluate Einstein's ideas. Schilpp's book includes Einstein's *Autobiographical Notes*, written in 1946 for this volume. Schilpp had hoped to give the book to Einstein on his birthday, but because of publishing delays, the presentation had to wait.

After he had turned seventy, the honors kept coming. In 1950 when Eleanor Roosevelt invited Einstein to contribute to her television program concerning the hydrogen bomb, Einstein told the television audience: "The idea of achieving security through national armament is, at the present state of military technique, a disastrous illusion."[71] In 1952 Einstein was invited to be the president of Israel, the Jewish state established in 1948. He declined, claiming that he was too old and too bad at politics. In 1953 Einstein received the Lord & Taylor Award and accepted it over radio: "As for words of warm praise addressed to me, I shall carefully refrain from disputing them."[72]

He received invitations to Bern, Switzerland, and to Berlin, Germany, for fiftieth-anniversary celebrations of his 1905 papers, but his poor health forced him to decline. Over the years he had been asked

Einstein in retirement. Retirement did not halt the honors and offers the great man received.

Einstein joy, what he suffered, and how he spent his days once he had retired. Retirement on Mercer Street took on simple routines. He still received a large amount of mail, which Helen Dukas sorted for him to answer. Einstein still loved music, but by 1949 he had given up playing his violin and played Bach and Mozart on his grand piano instead.

Ideas still came to him when he played music and did ordinary chores. He often stopped playing the piano, suddenly exclaiming that now he had got it, meaning he had found a scientific solution. Psychologist Julian Jaynes reported: "A close friend of Einstein's has told me that many of the physicist's greatest ideas came to him so suddenly while he was shaving that

Einstein spent many of his retirement hours with his sister Maja, with whom he remained very close until her death in 1951.

to make memorial statements celebrating Isaac Newton, Marie Curie, and many other famous scientists. Though his work in physics for the past thirty years had failed to produce new, major theories, Einstein was still the scientist of honor and the man of conscience.

Einstein's Private Life

While Einstein made his thoughts on science, philosophy, and politics public, he said little about his private affairs. Apart from a few comments about his childhood in his short *Autobiographical Notes*, he never wrote a personal autobiography. Yet letters and anecdotes show glimpses of what gave

After his retirement, Einstein's social life centered on his home. Here, he visits with some children, one of whom is his cousin, who have just arrived in the United States.

he had to move the blade of the straight razor very carefully each morning, lest he cut himself with surprise."[73]

In his retirement, Einstein's social life centered on his home and on walks around Princeton. He liked cats and had one of his own which he doted on. A Princeton resident told about the day he met Einstein on a walk, and Einstein wanted to see his new kittens. "He was dismayed when he saw that our neighbors were all people from the institute and said: 'Let's walk quickly. There are so many people here whose invitations I've declined. I hope they don't find out that I came to visit your kittens.'"[74]

Of the women who lived with Einstein, he felt closest to his sister Maja. Every evening they read together in the den, read aloud great works from world litera-ture. Those who heard the brother and sister speak together could hear the melodic sounds of the Swabian dialect in their speech. After 1946 Maja suffered from arteriosclerosis, a disease that impairs blood circulation. When she died in 1951, Einstein said in a letter to a cousin that he missed her more than he could easily explain. Though many friends and acquaintances described Einstein as a distant and aloof man, he also showed a warm and tender side.

Einstein had little warmth, however, for the Germans; he never forgave them. In 1933 he resented them for announcing publicly that they were taking away his citizenship when he had already given up both his German citizenship and his German passport. In 1946 after the German defeat in World War II, Einstein received

Einstein Street in Ulm

In 1946 the Germans restored Einstein's name to a street in his birthplace in Ulm, Germany, a street that the Ulm mayor had renamed during the Hitler era. Banesh Hoffmann explains the changes and quotes Einstein's response in Albert Einstein: Creator and Rebel:

"The house in Ulm where Einstein was born no longer stands. World War II reduced it to rubble. A street in Ulm had been named Einsteinstrasse. But the Nazis could not bear to see a Jew thus honored, especially one so great and one who by his whole life-style shone forth as a symbol of all that they sought to destroy. In Ulm the new Nazi mayor, on his first day in office, hastened to change the name Einsteinstrasse to Fichtestrasse, in honor of the eighteenth-century German philosopher and nationalist orator. Only with the defeat of the Nazis was the name Einsteinstrasse restored.

In letters written in 1946 Einstein said:

I had heard the droll story of the street names at the time and it caused me no little amusement. Whether anything has been changed since then I do not know, and I know even less when the next change will take place; but I do know how to restrain my curiosity. . . . I think that a neutral name such as "Windfahnenstrasse" [Weather Vane Street] would be better suited to the political mentality of the Germans and would make further rechristenings in the course of time unnecessary."

an invitation to rejoin the Bavarian Academy, but he declined, saying that he wanted nothing to do with Germans because they had slaughtered his Jewish brethren. In 1949 a letter asked him to renew ties with the Kaiser Wilhelm Institute. He sent this answer:

The crime of the Germans is truly the most abominable ever to be recorded in the history of the so-called civilized nations. The conduct of German intellectuals—seen as a group—was no better than that of a mob. And even now there is no indication of any regret or any real desire to repair whatever little may be left to restore after the gigantic murders. In the view of these circumstances I feel an irrepressible aversion to participating in anything that represents any aspect of public life in Germany.[75]

Einstein received many other invitations from Germans, but he never relented.

Opinions

Einstein never became a mellow old man. He retained his determined will, his independence of thought, and his commitment to causes until the end. At the beginning of his *Autobiographical Notes*, he said, "For the essential in the being of a man of my type lies precisely in *what* he thinks and *how* he thinks, not in what he does or suffers."[76] In his last years Einstein still spoke vigorously and wrote his views on world government and intellectual freedom.

Einstein said that the release of atomic energy had not created a new problem, but had made solving an existing one more urgent. He said as long as sovereign nations possessed great power, war was inevitable. A world government should control the secret of the atomic bomb. America should announce its readiness to give the secret to such a body. In an open letter to the General Assembly of the United Nations, Einstein said that the only guarantee for security and peace in this atomic age is the constant development of a supranational government and every citizen needs to "do everything in his power to strengthen the United Nations. . . . The United Nations now and world government eventually must serve one goal—the guarantee of the security, tranquility and the welfare of all mankind."[77] Though no nation took up Einstein's call for world government, he, nevertheless, continued to advocate the idea.

The McCarthy Era

Einstein advocated freedom of thought with the same vigor. During the early 1950s, Wisconsin senator Joseph McCarthy scrutinized government workers to see that they were not Communists. As paranoia

In the early 1950s, U.S. senator Joseph McCarthy led a paranoid attack on the civil liberties of Americans he suspected of radical views. Einstein spoke out against such suppression of freedoms.

Unified Field Theory Still Sought

The day before Einstein died, he asked for his papers, hoping to continue his effort to find a unified field theory. In The Advancement of Science, and Its Burdens, *Gerald Holton explains the effects of Einstein's efforts in field theory and comments on Einstein's failure:*

"Yet even as Einstein was hailed from about 1920 on as the very exemplar of what the human mind is capable of in science, he became more and more aware of what remained to be done than of what he had accomplished. Occasionally, Einstein thought he saw the end of his road on the horizon, close enough to reach it; but such periods lasted only briefly. His letters and essays document his growing realization that the program of unification itself might after all remain unreachable. . . .

As it has turned out, Einstein's exhortation to seek a unified *Weltbild* [world picture] is more coherent with the activities of many of today's best theoreticians than has been the case for the previous few decades. In a real sense, contemporary physicists, who use 'Grand Unification Program' quite simply as a technical term to identify their current version of that ancient quest, are recognizably following Einstein's general goal. This is not to say that threats to Einstein's own solution for the *Weltbild* have been overcome.

. . . Einstein did not live to see it come true in his time, and it may not come to be so in ours. If that is to be called a failure, it has to be the kind of noble failure that was also the fate of Newton."

within the country increased, many members of the academic community also were named as suspects and called to testify at public investigations. Einstein saw this activity as an affront to each individual's right to moral and intellectual freedom. Great masses of people, he said, fall victim more easily to a great lie than to a small one. When a teacher from Brooklyn, New York, refused to testify before the Congressional Committee, Einstein wrote a letter in his support and suggested he make the letter public. The letter, published in the *New York Times*, urged intellectuals to refuse to testify and be prepared for jail and economic ruin for the sake of the country's welfare. If many stood up, Einstein thought, success would come and freedom of thought would be preserved, but at the time the "lunatic fringe" was still in control.

Einstein wrote articles for newspapers and magazines about a host of topics. He explained how to educate children to

Officials from the New York state government and New York's Yeshiva University honor Einstein's seventy-fifth birthday by unveiling a model of the proposed Albert Einstein College of Medicine to be built at Yeshiva University.

think independently, that classical literature and a liberal-arts education are important, how imagination is crucial in scientific thought, and how science and religion are compatible. He explored the history and the persecution of the Jews. For a man who claimed to hate public attention, he did little to keep the public from knowing his opinions.

Realizing that his outspoken views often had little effect on events, Einstein frequently poked fun at himself. He said, "I still lose my temper dutifully about politics, but I no longer flap my wings—I only ruffle my feathers."[78] On one occasion he contrasted himself to Midas, the king of Phrygia in Greek mythology. When Midas touched something, it turned into gold; when Einstein touched something, it turned into a circus.

Failing Health

Throughout retirement Einstein's health, which had never completely returned after the 1928 breakdown, deteriorated enough to slow his activities. He had two operations, neither of which improved his condition. By his seventy-fifth birthday in 1954, he had begun reflecting on his life and work. His old friend Solovine suggested in a letter that Einstein must be looking back at the work of his lifetime with peace and satisfaction. Things, Einstein said, were not so bright. He said that his desire to seek unity explained why he had published so few papers and why his work had resulted in so many fruitless efforts.

To another friend he said that perhaps, after all, He (God) is a little malicious, implying that quantum mechanics may, after all, be correct. "I made one great mistake in my life," he said to chemist Linus Pauling, . . . "when I signed the letter to President Roosevelt recommending that atom bombs be made; but there was some justification—the danger that the Germans would make them."[79] Despite his sadness over these issues, Einstein never gave up in despair; he kept at his work as he had done in every time of difficulty or sorrow.

On Wednesday, April 13, 1955, Einstein was struck with severe pain. The doctor came on Thursday, and Einstein asked him how long death would take. The doctor suggested surgery, but Einstein refused. Einstein told Helen Dukas that the end had to come and that it did not matter when. Friday passed at home, but on Saturday the pain was so severe he agreed to go to the hospital because his care was too much for Helen. He had told her his last wishes. There was to be no funeral, no grave, and no monument. He directed that his brain be used for research, his body cremated, and the ashes scattered in an undisclosed place.

On Sunday the pain had lifted, and he wanted his glasses. His stepdaughter Margot, now in a wheelchair, was brought in to see him. His son Hans Albert and friend Otto Nathan arrived to be with him in his

---

Einstein's Apologies to the Japanese

Einstein agonized over the war and the atomic bomb, deeply regretting its destruction to the Japanese people. In an article originally published in 1952 in the Japanese magazine Kaizo *and reprinted in Einstein's* Ideas and Opinions, *he said:*

"My part in producing the atomic bomb consisted in a single act: I signed a letter to President Roosevelt, pressing the need for experiments on a large scale in order to explore the possibilities for the production of an atomic bomb.

I was fully aware of the terrible danger to mankind in case this attempt succeeded. But the likelihood that the Germans were working on the same problem with a chance of succeeding forced me to this step. I could do nothing else although I have always been a convinced pacifist. To my mind, to kill in war is not a whit better than to commit ordinary murder.

As long, however, as the nations are not resolved to abolish war through common actions and to solve their conflicts and protect their interests by peaceful decisions on a legal basis, they feel compelled to prepare for war. . . . Only the radical abolition of wars and of the threat of war can help. This is what one has to work for."

Einstein's study at the time of his death on April 18, 1955, was characteristically cluttered with papers, open books, his pipe, and equations on the blackboard.

last days. By late afternoon he felt better and asked for his papers and calculations, hoping to work on Monday, and they were brought to his bedside. On April 18, 1955, shortly after midnight, his breathing changed, and the nurse raised his bed. He quietly spoke words in German, but the nurse understood only English. Then he died. His words, so often misunderstood in life, were understood not at all in death. Reporters cabled millions of words out of Princeton, and in Germany an opera was being written about his life, soon to be presented in East Berlin.

9 Einstein's Influence

On the day that Albert Einstein died, his death in no way represented an end to his influence. Many scientists have spoken about Einstein's overall effect on the twentieth century. Science historians have cited the huge number of research projects his work has generated. They have listed technology that has indirectly developed as a result of Einstein's discoveries. Artists, literary critics, psychologists, philosophers, and theologians have explained how Einstein affected their fields. Sorting out what ef-fect his work has had becomes increasingly difficult as the results snowball from Einstein's original work.

Einstein published some three hundred papers in the physical sciences, but his 1905 papers and his 1916 general relativity theory are the ones that identify him as the most important scientist of the twentieth century. Physicist Heinz Pagels said that Einstein "fathered" twentieth-century physics. Science historian Gerald Holton called him "a great revolutionary"; physi-

Dr. Hans Sprecker, director of the Ulm city archives, displays a poster advertising the centennial of Einstein's birth there in 1879.

The Maker of a Universe

In 1966 Cornelius Lanczos honored Einstein in a series of six lectures published in Albert Einstein and the Cosmic World Order. *In the essay entitled "Summary and Outlook," he quoted a tribute written earlier by British playwright and satirist George Bernard Shaw:*

"'Newton knew that the universe consisted of bodies in motion, and that none of them moved in straight lines, nor ever could. But an Englishman was not daunted by facts. To explain why all the lines in his rectilinear [consisting of straight lines] universe were bent, he invented a force called gravitation and thus erected a complete British universe and established it as a religion which was devoutly believed in for 300 years. The book of this Newtonian religion was not that oriental magic thing, the Bible. It was that British and matter-of-fact thing a Bradshaw. [A Bradshaw is a British railway timetable.] It gives the stations of all the heavenly bodies, their distances, the rates at which they are travelling, and the hour at which they reach eclipsing points or crash into the earth like Sirius [the brightest star in the sky]. Every item is precise, ascertained, absolute and English.

'Three hundred years after its establishment a young professor rises calmly in the middle of Europe and says to our astronomers: "Gentlemen: if you will observe the next eclipse of the sun carefully, you will be able to explain what is wrong with the perihelion of Mercury." The civilized Newtonian world replies that, if the dreadful thing is true, if the eclipse makes good the blasphemy, the next thing the young professor will do is to question the existence of gravitation. The young professor smiles and says that gravitation is a very useful hypothesis, . . . but that personally he can do without it. He is asked to explain how, if there is no gravitation, the heavenly bodies do not move in straight lines and run clear out of the universe. He replies that no explanation is needed because the universe is not rectilinear and exclusively British; it is curvilinear. The Newtonian universe thereupon drops dead and is supplanted by an Einsteinian universe. Einstein has not challenged the facts of science but the axioms of science, and science has surrendered to the challenge.'"

cist and biographer Phillip Frank said Einstein was the "nucleus" of the revolution. Physicist and astronomer Timothy Ferris called Einstein a "gadfly," searching for a new system. Of gadflies, Ferris said, "That is their job—to punch holes in belief systems and let the light shine through, awakening the rest of us."[80] C.P. Snow suggested that the twentieth century would somehow have been different had Einstein not existed. Physicist Cornelius Lanczos summed up Einstein's importance in one of his lectures:

> He has given us a new picture of the universe and he has demonstrated the power of inspired abstract thinking. Never before had any human being attained such marvelous insights into the inner heart of the physical universe. Never before would it have been possible even to hope that some day our minds may clearly recognize the master plan according to which the universe is constructed. What he accomplished in a single lifetime is stupendous and a sufficient basis for research for hundreds of years to come. In an era of unprecedented aggressiveness and destruction he held up a mirror to the human mind and demonstrated its greatness and its boundless possibilities if turned toward inspired constructive reasoning. He thus occupies a place in the history of civilization which is unique and may never be duplicated.[81]

While the testimony of reputable scientists is one measure of Einstein's importance, the amount of significant research his theory generated is another. Einstein's light quanta theory and his special relativity theory form the basis for the whole of quantum mechanics—the branch of nuclear physics developed by Rutherford, Bohr, de Broglie, Schrödinger, Heisenberg, Dirac, Born, and Fermi. "But because he was Einstein, just having him say that this was an important idea automatically got people to pay attention to it and got these ideas into the mainstream of physics much more quickly than would have happened otherwise."[82]

Moreover, Einstein's general relativity opened up a new vision of the universe that formed the basis for cosmology, the study of the entire universe. The theory also provided the mathematical tools for studying the origin of the universe, the big bang theory. Physicists continue to try to measure gravitational waves, the one prediction in general relativity not yet verified. In the summer of 1992, physicists from the California Institute of Technology and the Massachusetts Institute of Technology started a cooperative venture to build a pair of observatories designed to detect gravitational waves. Moreover, science historian Gerald Holton pointed out that two decades after Einstein's death, physicists began making advances toward a unification theory, the theory that consumed Einstein's later years.

Einstein's Impact

In 1977 two research scholars working for the Institute for Scientific Information, Tony Cawkell and Eugene Garfield, analyzed Einstein's impact on science. They studied the *Science Citation Index* to see how many published works cited Einstein as a direct or indirect influence. For 1977 they found that 105 articles had the word "Einstein" in the title. They found that

Einstein Inspires Artists

Artists and intellectuals from many fields viewed the world and their work in a new way as a result of Einstein's theories. In an essay entitled "Einstein and Art," Philip Courtenay explains what he calls "a major transformation of vision." His essay is published in Einstein: The First Hundred Years:

"When we consider the work of Einstein it is as if, even now, we look at ourselves and the world in a radically new way. Any scientific revolution reflects a major transformation of vision; as a new world view it profoundly affects the consciousness of those aware of its substance and implications. And the transformation of vision that accompanies a scientific revolution is not limited to the scientific community. Conversely, the character of new scientific theory is determined from the matrix [the situation within which it originates or develops] of possibilities allowed by a culture, the culture that nurtures it. So the interplay of the social forces that shape a culture is vital to our discussion of the parallels between Einstein's theories and the contemporary revolution in the visual arts. Both the domain of intellect and realm of subjective experience are formed by our perception of the world, and perception itself is governed by our sense faculties. . . .

Today the world 'relativity' resonates with images of time and space. This is a measure of Einstein's effect upon our thinking. The work of certain artists touches us in a similar way. We speak of physics 'since Einstein' in the same manner as in the visual arts it is common to talk of painting 'since Cézanne'. . . . In their different ways, Einstein and Cézanne show us a profoundly novel, holistic way of seeing and experiencing the world."

452 cited Einstein within the article. They concluded:

Considering the time which has elapsed since Einstein published his most important articles, the direct influence and on-going interest in his work is quite extraordinary. We have examined a sufficiently large sample of the citing articles to note that a high proportion of them stem directly from his research or contain discussions of developments prompted by his various theories. The number of these articles, their interdisciplinary character and the comments made by their authors confirm the outstanding influence and the direct impact of Einstein's work on today's science.[83]

Effect on Technology

While scientists know the importance of Einstein's theories, the ordinary person on the street is usually ignorant of Einstein's influence. People know his name, but when asked what he contributed to science, they often answer that they never were very good in mathematics or that he discovered something important like relativity. People who know little about Einstein may be surprised to learn how many objects in their daily lives developed, directly or indirectly, out of Einstein's theories.

For example, it is his theory that makes a television camera work, that allows for the optical soundtrack of a motion picture, the photocomposition of newspapers and books, and communication by telephone over a modern fiber cable. His theory made the laser possible for medical work and computer printers. Einstein's theories made possible power generators and precision clocks used to chart the course of ships and planes. Einstein's theories also appear in calculators, computers, transistor radios, ignition systems, and even in the process for making vitamin pills and pharmaceutical drugs.

Effect on Art

Furthermore, Einstein's influence extends to the arts, not because his theories are about art, but because his new ideas inspired artists to create in new ways. Relativity, space-time, curved space, particle-wave, mass-energy, all concepts in Einstein's theories, jarred artists' imaginations and gave them new vision. For example, engineer R. Buckminster Fuller built geodesic domes that imitated Einstein's concept of curved space. Einstein's concepts are reflected in new forms and new kinds of composition in the works of sculptors and painters. Cubism in painting is an example. Moreover, poets and writers have found inspiration for new plots and characters and have re-

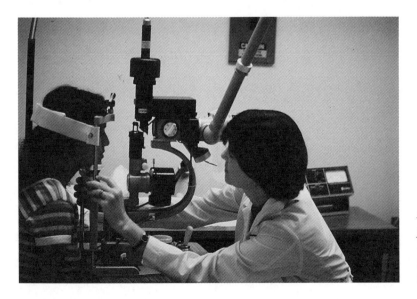

An eye surgeon prepares a patient for laser treatment. The discovery of lasers was made possible by Einstein's theories of light.

(Left) R. Buckminster Fuller invented the geodesic dome using Einstein's ideas of curved space. He stands here in front of his geodesic dome house. (Right) Einstein's new way of looking at the world inspired the painting style known as cubism, here represented by a work of Pablo Picasso.

ferred to Einstein in their writing. Poets Robert Frost, e.e. cummings, T.S. Eliot, and writers Jean-Paul Sartre, William Faulkner, and Tom Stoppard all referred to Einstein in their works. American poet William Carlos Williams illustrated in a humorous way one writer's reference to Einstein:

St. Francis Einstein of the Daffodils

April Einstein
. . . has come among the daffodils
shouting
that flowers and men
were created
relatively equal.[84]

Bernstein said that the magnitude of Einstein's creativity is really beyond explanation. To this opinion physicist Leopold Infeld added:

> Einstein is unlike anyone else. And perhaps this simple fact is the real clue to his fame. The real clue is not the spectacular discovery of the bending of light rays. If this were so, why should this fame persist in a quickly changing world that forgets today its idols of yesterday? It must rather be his inner greatness, which the people of the world somehow sense and need for their comfort.[85]

Notes

Introduction: Revolutionizing Science

1. Phillip Frank, *Einstein: His Life and Times*. Translated from a German manuscript by George Rosen and edited and revised by Shuichi Kusaka, with a new introduction. New York: Alfred A. Knopf, 1953.

Chapter 1: Childhood: 1879-1895

2. Ronald W. Clark, *Einstein: The Life and Times*. New York: The World Publishing Company, 1971.

3. Banesh Hoffmann, with the collaboration of Helen Dukas, *Albert Einstein: Creator and Rebel*. New York: Penguin Books, 1972.

4. Albert Einstein, *Autobiographical Notes*, 1949. Reprint. Translated and edited by Paul Arthur Schilpp. La Salle, IL: Open Court Publishing Company, 1979.

5. Frank, *Einstein*.

6. Hoffmann, *Albert Einstein*.

7. Clark, *Einstein*.

8. Einstein, *Notes*.

9. Hoffmann, *Albert Einstein*.

10. Einstein, *Notes*.

11. Einstein, *Notes*.

12. Hoffmann, *Albert Einstein*.

13. Hoffmann, *Albert Einstein*.

Chapter 2: University Education and Career Plans: 1895-1905

14. Heinz R. Pagels, *The Cosmic Code: Quantum Physics as the Language of Nature*. New York: Simon and Schuster, 1982.

15. Anton Reiser, *Albert Einstein: A Biographical Portrait*. New York: Albert and Charles Boni, 1930.

16. Clark, *Einstein*.

17. Clark, *Einstein*.

18. Hoffmann, *Albert Einstein*.

19. Reiser, *Albert Einstein*.

Chapter 3: The 1905 Papers and Success: 1905-1914

20. Clark, *Einstein*.

21. Albert Einstein, *Out of My Later Years*. Westport, CT: Greenwood Press, 1970.

22. Pagels, *The Cosmic Code*.

23. Hoffmann, *Albert Einstein*.

24. Einstein, *Notes*.

25. Hoffmann, *Albert Einstein*.

26. Einstein, *Out of My Later Years*.

27. Frank, *Einstein*.

28. Frank, *Einstein*.

29. Reiser, *Albert Einstein*.

30. Frank, *Einstein*.

31. Frank, *Einstein*.

32. Frank, *Einstein*.

33. Frank, *Einstein*.

Chapter 4: Berlin, General Relativity, and Fame: 1914-1920

34. Reiser, *Albert Einstein*.

35. Clark, *Einstein*.

36. Timothy Ferris, *Coming of Age in the Milky Way*. New York: William Morrow and Company, Inc., 1988.

37. Hoffmann, *Albert Einstein*.

38. Stephen W. Hawking, *A Brief History of Time: From the Big Bang to Black Holes*. New York: Bantam Books, 1988.

39. Ferris, *Coming of Age*.

40. Clark, *Einstein*.

41. Pagels, *The Cosmic Code*.

42. Clark, *Einstein*.

43. Frank, *Einstein*.

44. Leopold Infeld, "To Albert Einstein on His 75th Birthday." In *Einstein: The First Hundred Years*, edited by Maurice Goldsmith, Alan Mackay, and James Woudhuysen. New York: Pergamon Press, 1980.

Chapter 5: Recognition, Misconceptions, and Causes: 1920-1933

45. Reiser, *Albert Einstein*.

46. Frank, *Einstein*.

47. Clark, *Einstein*.

48. C.P. Snow, "Einstein." In *Einstein: The First Hundred Years*, edited by Maurice Goldsmith, Alan Mackay, and James Woudhuysen. New York: Pergamon Press, 1980.

49. Frank, *Einstein*.

50. Frank, *Einstein*.

51. Reiser, *Albert Einstein*.

52. Albert Einstein, *Ideas and Opinions*. Based on *Mein Weltbild*. Edited by Carl Seelig and other sources. New York: Crown Publishers, 1954.

Chapter 6: Quiet Life, the Rise of Hitler, and Departure from Berlin: 1920-1933

53. Reiser, *Albert Einstein*.

54. Frank, *Einstein*.

55. Clark, *Einstein*.

56. Einstein, *Ideas*.

57. Frank, *Einstein*.

58. Clark, *Einstein*.

59. Einstein, *Ideas*.

60. Ferris, *Coming of Age*.

61. Frank, *Einstein*.

Chapter 7: America and the Institute for Advanced Study: 1933-1945

62. Clark, *Einstein*.

63. Clark, *Einstein*.

64. Clark, *Einstein*.

65. Gerald Holton, *The Advancement of Science, and Its Burdens: The Jefferson Lecture and Other Essays*. Cambridge: Cambridge University Press, 1986.

66. Einstein, *Out of My Later Years*.

67. Clark, *Einstein*.

68. Clark, *Einstein*.

Chapter 8: Retirement Years: 1945-1955

69. Einstein, *Ideas*.

70. Einstein, *Ideas*.

71. Einstein, *Ideas*.

72. Einstein, *Ideas*.

73. Julian Jaynes, *The Origin of Consciousness in the Breakdown of the Bicameral Mind*. Boston: Houghton Mifflin Co., 1976.

74. Hoffmann, *Albert Einstein*.

75. Hoffmann, *Albert Einstein*.

76. Einstein, *Notes*.

77. Einstein, *Out of My Later Years*.

78. Clark, *Einstein*.

79. Clark, *Einstein*.

Chapter 9: Einstein's Influence

80. Timothy Ferris, *The Mind's Sky: Human Intelligence in a Cosmic Context*. New York: Bantam Books, 1992.

81. Cornelius Lanczos, *Albert Einstein and the Cosmic World Order*. New York: John Wiley & Sons, Inc., 1965.

82. Jeremy Bernstein and Gerald Feinberg, *Science and the Human Imagination: Albert Einstein*. Papers and discussions. Publication of the Leverton Lecture Series, edited by Charles Angoff, no. 5. Cranbury, NJ: Associated University Presses, Inc., 1978.

83. Tony Cawkell and Eugene Garfield, "Assessing Einstein's Impact on Today's Science by Citation Analysis." In *Einstein: The First Hundred Years*, edited by Maurice Goldsmith, Alan Mackay, and James Woudhuysen. New York: Pergamon Press, 1980.

84. Holton, *Advancement*.

85. Infeld, "To Albert Einstein."

For Further Reading

E.N. da C Andrade, *Sir Isaac Newton*. Science Study Series. Garden City, NY: Anchor Books, Doubleday, 1954. Tells about Newton's life and theories and places him in history.

Pamela Zanin Bradbury, *Albert Einstein*. The Great American Series. New York: Julian Messner, 1988. An account of key events in Einstein's life, illustrated with drawings by James Seward.

William Cahn, *Einstein: A Pictorial Biography*. New York: The Citadel Press, 1955. A good collection of photos from Einstein's life, accompanied by short texts.

Milton Dank, *Albert Einstein*. Impact Biographies. New York: Franklin Watts, 1983. Presents Einstein's life and work, with further explanation of theories in appendices.

Aylesa Forsee, *Albert Einstein: Theoretical Physicist*. New York: The Macmillan Company, 1963. Begins with Einstein as a student and tells of his life, humanitarian causes, and contributions to science.

Nigel Hunter, *Einstein*. New York: Bookwright Press, 1987. Brief account of life, politics, and causes, illustrated by Richard Hook.

Elma Ehrlich Levinger, *Albert Einstein*. New York: Julian Messner, 1949. Fictionalized account of Einstein's life from his childhood through his work at the Institute for Advanced Study, with foreword by Einstein's son Hans Albert.

Alan Lightman, *Einstein's Dreams*. New York: Pantheon Books, 1993. A novel using Einstein and his theories as a metaphor to show meaning of time.

Joseph Schwartz and Michael McGuinness, *Einstein for Beginners*. New York: Pantheon Books, 1979. Cartoon drawings presented in comic-book style explaining Einstein's personal history and his theories.

Antonina Vallentin, *The Drama of Albert Einstein*. Translated by Moura Budberg. Garden City, NY: Doubleday, 1954. Written with humor and drama by a woman who knew Einstein.

Works Consulted

Marcia Bartusiak, "Einstein's Unfinished Symphony," *Discover*, August 1989. An explanation of gravitational waves, Einstein's fourth prediction in general relativity, and an update on attempts to verify the prediction.

Jeremy Bernstein, and Gerald Feinberg, *Science and the Human Imagination: Albert Einstein*. Papers and discussions. Publication of the Leverton Lecture Series, edited by Charles Angoff, no. 5. Cranbury, NJ: Associated University Presses, 1978. A series of lectures giving a tribute to Einstein and explaining how Einstein combined science and imagination to develop his theories.

William Blanpied. *See* Goldsmith entry.

Lee Calcraft. *See* Goldsmith entry.

Tony Cawkell and Eugene Garfield. *See* Goldsmith entry.

Bill Chaitkin. *See* Goldsmith entry.

Ronald W. Clark, *Einstein: The Life and Times*. New York: The World Publishing Company, 1971. A thorough biography of Einstein, providing the reader with a wealth of details and background.

Philip Courtenay. *See* Goldsmith entry.

Albert Einstein, *Autobiographical Notes*. 1949. Reprint. Translated and edited by Paul Arthur Schilpp. La Salle, IL: Open Court Publishing Company, 1979. A few impressions from childhood and an explanation of what and how Einstein thought.

——————, *Ideas and Opinions*. Based on *Mein Westbild*. Edited by Carl Seelig and other sources. New York: Crown Publishers, 1954. A collection of speeches, articles, and letters, in which Einstein explains his philosophy and political ideals up to the early 1930s.

——————, *Out of My Later Years*. New York: Philosophical Library, 1950. Reprint. Westport, CT: Greenwood Press, 1970. A collection of speeches, articles, and letters, in which Einstein explains his philosophy and political ideals after the early 1930s.

Timothy Ferris, *Coming of Age in the Milky Way*. New York: William Morrow and Company, 1988. An astronomer and physicist's explanation of twentieth-century physics and cosmology.

——————, *The Mind's Sky: Human Intelligence in a Cosmic Context*. New York: Bantam Books, 1992. An imaginative exploration of the relationship between the human mind and the universe.

Phillip Frank, *Einstein: His Life and Times*. Translated from a German manuscript by George Rosen and edited and revised by Shuichi Kusaka, with a new introduction. New York: Alfred A. Knopf, 1953. An account of Einstein's personal life and theories by a physicist who knew Einstein and filled the position in Zurich when Einstein resigned.

Maurice Goldsmith, Alan Mackay, and James Woudhuysen, eds., *Einstein: The First Hundred Years*. New York: Pergamon Press, 1980. A collection of essays commemorating the hundredth anniversary of Einstein's birth. Essays cover tributes to Einstein's achievements, his personal life, and his influence on science, art, and culture.

Stephen W. Hawking, *A Brief History of Time: From the Big Bang to Black Holes*. New York: Bantam Books, 1988. An explanation of modern astrophysics and the nature of time.

Banesh Hoffmann, with the collaboration of Helen Dukas, *Albert Einstein: Creator and Rebel*. New York: Penguin Books, 1972. A presentation of Einstein's personal life and science, emphasizing the importance of Einstein's independence by a physics colleague from the institute in New Jersey with the help of Einstein's secretary.

Gerald Holton, *The Advancement of Science, and Its Burdens: The Jefferson Lecture and Other Essays*. Cambridge: Cambridge University Press, 1986. A science historian's account of Einstein's theories and ideas in the context of twentieth-century scientific achievements.

Leopold Infeld. *See* Goldsmith entry.

Julian Jaynes, *The Origin of Consciousness in the Breakdown of the Bicameral Mind*. Boston: Houghton Mifflin, 1976. A psychologist's exploration of intuition, imagination, creativity, and thought.

Cornelius Lanczos, *Albert Einstein and the Cosmic World Order*. New York: John Wiley & Sons, 1965. A series of six lectures on Einstein's greatness, his theories, and his influence.

Heinz R. Pagels, *The Cosmic Code: Quantum Physics as the Language of Nature*. New York: Simon and Schuster, 1982. A history of science and the atom, including an explanation of how Einstein's theories provided a breakthrough in the development of quantum mechanics.

Anton Reiser, *Albert Einstein: A Biographical Portrait*. New York: Albert and Charles Boni, 1930. A personal account of Einstein's life before he moved to America, written by Einstein's son-in-law.

Joseph Rotblat. *See* Goldsmith entry.

Paul Arthur Schilpp, ed., *Albert Einstein: Philosopher-Scientist*. Two volumes. New York: Harper and Brothers, 1949. A collection of scholarly essays about Einstein's ideas and theories, written for his seventieth birthday celebration.

C.P. Snow. *See* Goldsmith entry.

T. Walter Wallbank and Alastair M. Taylor, *Civilization: Past and Present*. Two volumes. Chicago: Scott, Foresman and Company, 1949. A general history of the Western world.

Index

Picture Credits

Cover photo by UPI/Bettmann

AIP Emilio Segrè Visual Archives, 59

AIP Emilio Segrè Visual Archives, Fritz Reiche Collection, 61

AIP Niels Bohr Library, 78

AP/Wide World Photos, 7, 49, 52, 53, 68, 76, 82, 90, 92 (both), 93 (right), 95, 96, 98, 101, 102 (top), 105, 109, 110, 115 (both)

Beckman Laser Institute, 114

The Bettmann Archive, 32, 47, 57, 60, 64 (bottom), 70, 85

Brown Brothers, 36 (top), 56

Deutschland Erwacht/Simon Wiesenthal Center Archives, Los Angeles, CA, 86

By permission of the Hebrew University of Jerusalem, Israel, 9 (both), 10 (both), 20, 30 (bottom), 48, 62, 102 (bottom)

Historical Pictures/Stock Montage, 26, 36 (bottom), 65, 73, 91

Institute International de Physique Solvay, courtesy AIP Emilio Segrè Visual Archives, 46

Library of Congress, 8, 23, 34

© Magnum/Erich Lessing, 38, 43

The Mansell Collection, 51

NASA, 18, 58

National Archives, 83 (top), 88

North Wind Picture Archives, 12, 14, 15, 16

Smithsonian Institution, 99

UPI/Bettmann, 28, 64 (top), 67, 81, 83 (bottom), 84, 93 (left), 103, 107

Wayland Publishers Ltd., 21, 29, 30 (top), 72, 75, 87

About the Author

After several years of teaching British literature, Clarice Swisher now devotes her time to writing and editing. She is the author of *The Beginning of Language* and *Relativity* in Greenhaven Press's Great Mystery series. She lives in Saint Paul, Minnesota.